TO

SEEK

AND

SAVE

THE GOSPEL OF LUKE

• STEPHEN GOSLING •

www.hispubg.com
A division of HISpecialists, llc

HIS Publishing Group
4310 Wiley Post Rd., Suite 201D
Addison, Texas 75001
info@hispubg.com

Library of Congress Control Number: 2016916858
Perfect Bound Edition ISBN-13: 978-0-578-18536-1
Electronic Edition ISBN-13: 978-0-578-18700-6

Cover Illustration by Leon Ducker Sr.

Comentary on the Book of Luke/Stephen Gosling—1st ed.
10 9 8 7 6 5 4 3 2 1

Printed in the United States of America

ADVANCED PRAISE FOR TO SEEK AND SAVE

Steve Gosling has offered to the church a study of Luke's Gospel that will be of help to leaders and participants of adult Bible studies. It would likewise be a welcome companion for private devotional use. Using the theme of the great promises of God, this study walks the reader through Luke's narrative with confidence and purpose. Evident on every page is the author's passion and love for the subject matter and especially for the Lord Jesus, to whom Luke bears witness and invites us to know.

—Dan Griswold
Senior Pastor at Trinity Reformed Church in Rochester NY
Dan holds a PhD in Systematic Theology from SMU and is
the author of *The Triune Eternal—God's Relationship to
Time in Theology of Karl Barth*

Many have written about the Gospel of Luke. On my personal bookshelf, I have numerous commentaries and Biblical Exegesis that lend scholastic insight into the nuances of its intended audience and meaning. However, Steve Gosling writes from a different perspective. Gosling offers inspiration to his writing of this commentary on the Book of Luke. Drawing from Biblical commentaries and other writers he adds the inspiration of the Holy Spirit as he brings together his thoughts into an easy to read and understand commentary. This book is made available to anyone who just wants to dive in a little deeper and grasp a better understanding for themselves—always allowing the God who is still speaking to speak again, and again as the Holy Spirit guides personal study and interpretation. I pray that anyone who reads it will open themselves us, like Steve to what the Spirit was saying through Luke and how we might make that relevant today.

—The Reverend Dr. Neil G. Cazares-Thomas
Senior Pastor Cathedral of Hope United Church of Christ

To Seek and Save is beautifully written. Steve Gosling has such a way with words. I was completely engaged and inspired by the way he took me through the whole of Luke's story. And I felt the tension building in me as I read his interpretation, his commentary and his exhortation to listen well to Jesus' invitation to follow completely. Many of the commentaries I read for my work are so scholarly and dry, but this one is accessible, inspiring and even, dare I say it, exciting! I recommend his commentary to any person interested in knowing more about Jesus, who he is, what he came for and what it means to say, "I am a Jesus Follower!" Thank you for this great work, Steve!

—Reverend Mary Beth Hardesty-Crouch
Senior Pastor Vista Ridge United Methodist Church

TABLE OF CONTENTS

PREFACE

B ecause I have led the study of the book of Luke several times at church, many people have recommended that I write a book using the material from the class. I always dismissed these suggestions, first because I did not consider myself a writer and second because I did not have the time to devote to such an endeavor.

Early in my life, I thought I wanted to be a preacher. Later, God made it clear He wanted me to be a teacher, not a preacher. I was blessed to have two wonderful mentors at the beginning: Trent Humphries and Rev. Paul Morrell. In the last 24 years, I have taught adult Bible study, Disciple Bible Study, and various other types of classes at the churches I've attended.

Yes, I decided to write this book. No, I am not a writer, but I have learned that if God gives us a task, He will provide what is needed to accomplish it. I did ask God to help me understand if writing this book was just a good idea from people, something I wanted to do, or truly a calling from Him. We are not always fortunate enough to receive clarity in such a timely manner, but this time, not only was God faithful to tell me that I should write the book, but also He helped me understand how it would unfold.

This book is not intended to be an academic tome. It is, rather, more like capturing the accumulated content of the classes I taught over the years, including the valuable input from learned students. These classes were not short. In fact, the normal time for a Luke class averaged 18 months. The book is intended to be used for adult Bible study, a resource book for Bible study teachers, or simply a book for someone who wants to know more about the Gospel of Luke.

The book is divided into the same chapters as it is conventionally presented in most Bibles. To understand the commentary in context, it is highly recommended the readers read a chapter in their Bible, followed by the corresponding chapter in this commentary.

The sources are varied but are generally secondary, such as Barclay's or Matthew Henry's commentaries, along with books by Charles Swindoll and others. Various study Bibles were used of different translations as well the many resources available in Logos. A lot is simply "making sense" of Luke after studying these resources for years, getting into Luke's head, and understanding why and how he wrote—what was behind the writing.

All this research is great and makes for an interesting book, but it is useless without the last step (short of being subjected to the editor!), which is the inspiration of the Holy Spirit. The final pass through the text was opened through prayer to God for Him to guide me through changes, editions, and additions.

God is good and allowed the manuscript to take shape pretty much according to plan, though He occasionally interjected inspiration during the process prior to the last stage. The result is a work combining years of effort on my part and the inspiration of the Holy Spirit.

Glory to God!
Stephen Gosling

May the love of the Father,
The peace of Jesus Christ and
The power of the Holy Spirit
Be with you.

INTRODUCTION

L uke is the one gospel in the Bible written by someone who was not an apostle. He did not live with Jesus for three years; therefore, he did not know him personally, hear his teachings, witness the miracles, suffer the trauma of his passion, or experience the life-changing baptism of the Holy Spirit at Pentecost in Jerusalem. Yet his gospel story is rich in detail and remarkably consistent with the other Gospels. What we do know is that Luke was a physician. Paul tells us that in Colossians 4:14. He traveled with Paul, starting with Paul's second missionary journey, was incarcerated with Paul in Rome, and apparently was with Paul when many others had left him (2 Timothy 4:11).

We also know Luke was a Gentile and well educated. The Greek, in which he wrote the book, is outstanding, at times bordering on classical. His perspective throughout the book is clearly through the lens of a Gentile, seeing the salvation story as applicable to everyone and not limited to only the Jews. Luke's writing style is so sophisticated that he varies it according to the setting of the story. When writing about a Jewish scene, he reverts to a more Semitic language, such as when he writes about Peter in a Jewish locale.

From the beginning, Luke clearly states his purpose for writing, which was to provide Theophilus a comprehensive story of the gospel so he could fully understand the truths he had been taught.

If Luke were not one of the disciples walking with Jesus, how did he present such a detailed portrait of Christ's life? Four methods were used. First, he spoke with the living apostles, who were Jesus' witnesses (Luke 24:48). Second, he was with Paul for years, an incredibly valuable source of information, both about the gospel story and, just as important, Hebrew culture and history. Third, by the time Luke wrote his book, Mark's gospel had been written, so he had access to it for corroboration, as well as the document known as Q, a collection of Jesus' sayings, put together by an unknown source, which pre-dates all the gospels. Fourth, Luke performed his own extensive investigations. More on the fourth method later.

So how did Luke support himself during this time of investigation? There are two possibilities. Because Theophilus was likely a man of wealth, he could have been Luke's patron, commissioning him for this task. God does have a pattern of providing for His ministry. Joanna, the wife of Cuza, helped support Jesus and the disciples. Cuza was the manager of Herod's household, so she had access to funds. Likewise, Lydia, being a person of wealth and a dealer in purple cloth, helped support Paul and the other disciples.

The other possibility, however, is that Luke paid his own way. We know he was a physician, so it would be relatively easy for him to ply his trade wherever he went. Working to support oneself would be consistent with Paul's way of doing things, setting up his tent-making wherever he went so he would not be a burden on those he was sent to serve.

> 2 Thessalonians 3:8
> Nor did we eat anyone's food without paying for it. On the contrary, we worked night and day, laboring and toiling so that we would not be a burden to any of you.

Most scholars agree on the general themes running through Luke, though there are many minor themes threaded within as well:

- The universal application of salvation to include the Gentiles as well as the Jews.
- Emphasis on prayer.
- Emphasis on the role of women.

- Focus on the poor. Others disenfranchised by society received special attention, but the poor are singled out repeatedly.
- Joy and praise, both at the reception of the Good News and then acting upon it.
- Concern for sinners. This concept could be the central theme of Luke, at least according to Jesus, who summarized his mission in one simple sentence in Luke 19:10: **"For the Son of Man came to seek and to save what was lost."**
- Jesus' repeated use of phrase "Son of Man."
- Emphasis on the Holy Spirit.

When did Luke write his book? Basically, we do not know for certain. The preponderance of the evidence, however, points to the time shortly after his internment with Paul in Rome. The two had already spent much time traveling together. You might have heard it said, "You really get to know someone when you travel with them." All the truer in those days! I would suggest being in the same jail cell enhanced their relationship even more. It would also appear the book was written prior to the fall of Jerusalem in 70 AD, for all references to its destruction are future tense.

When Luke wrote is important because it addresses a key point about Luke's theology, which is remarkably similar to Paul's. There are differences, of course, but those are more for the study of theologians who like to dwell on the finer points not substantially significant to the general orientation. The differences can be simply chalked up to the expected differences between two people of the same view who express that view differently. The same holds true of the four gospels, and it is true of the theology of Paul and Luke. As much as he contributed to Luke's gospel, Paul could well be the co-author of it.

It was with Paul's deep understanding as a Pharisee, an educated Jew steeped in the Hebrew scripture, that Luke could comprehend:

- The context of Christ being the climax of history as foretold by the prophets.

- The relationship of the Jewish festivals and the events in Jesus' life, especially during his last week.
- The individual's responsibility for his or her own salvation. This final point is key. Although Luke maintains strongly the universal application of salvation, that it is available to all for all time, it is up to each person to accept it or reject it. That God knows who will or won't does not restrict our free choice. This theology of the elect, predestined for salvation, is consistent through Paul's writings (granted, getting stronger in his later writings,) and the Gospel of Luke.

Luke's gospel also includes God's great promises. These can be found throughout all of scripture, from Genesis through The Revelation to John, and woven incredibly consistently through the books of History, Prophecy, Poetry, Gospels, and Letters. Their meaning may be historically specific when written, yet we gain a new understanding later with the benefit of additional context of hindsight. God's Word and Wisdom are often revealed in layers over time, as are His promises. To Him, all time is now, and His Word does not change, only our understanding of it.

The promises give us a glimpse of God's glory by seeing the fruits of His grace. God didn't have to make these promises but did out of the overwhelming love He has for us. We know this grace through Jesus Christ, the subject of Luke's gospel. Grace, the gift from God, which we do not deserve, is freely given through His promises.

John 3:16
"For God so loved the world that he gave his one and only Son, that whoever believes in him shall not perish but have eternal life."

John 1:17
For the law was given through Moses; grace and truth came through Jesus Christ.

GOD'S GREAT PROMISES

1. God faithfully prepares His people for their future.
2. God faithfully provides for His people.
3. God faithfully protects His people.
4. God faithfully promises peace for His people, not peace as the world understands it, but peace that truly surpasses all comprehension.
5. God faithfully promises His presence. This promise is the very truth of Who He is. He is I AM, I AM Being, I AM Becoming, Immanuel, God with us.
6. God faithfully offers His people His promises. They are scattered like glitter throughout the Bible; some are conditional, some are not. All are unilateral.

Luke's writing is also inclusive. Most readers find themselves somewhere in the story. He introduces multiple characters in various settings. He is a masterful storyteller. At some point, each reader or listener will identify with one of the people and be drawn in and make the story his or her own. Luke is indeed an instrument of the Holy Spirit. He works his craft well and leaves the rest to Him.

THE GOSPEL OF LUKE

CHAPTER ONE

L uke begins his letter in the formal style of his day This format tells us right away Luke is well educated, writing in excellent Greek and maintaining the academic form of his time for a letter such as this one. He is writing to Theophilus, a common Greek name at the time, meaning "one who loves God." That he is addressed as "most excellent" probably indicates Theophilus is a high-ranking Roman official, such as a governor.

It is clear that Theophilus trusted Luke and would accept his version of the gospel. The foundation for witnessing the gospel to another person is a solid, personal relationship with that individual. Such a foundation must be established first with the element of trust in place, so when the truth is presented, it is seen with an open heart and mind. This truth provides fertile soil in which the Holy Spirit can work (Luke 8:11 – 15).

Others had written their own versions of the story of Jesus. It is interesting that Luke referred to his story rather obliquely as "account of the things that have been fulfilled among us," meaning Luke's own gospel story of Jesus of Nazareth would become obvious to those reading his letter. His emphasis here, however, is that the truth of this story, both as told by others before him and now told by himself, is prophecy fulfilled. Even though Luke was a Gentile, by the time he wrote this account, he had been around Jews who had converted to Christianity for several years and had come to appreciate their heritage. It is obvious, as we will see, that Luke had also learned the Hebrew Scriptures, for he referred to them throughout his letter. Although Matthew's gospel is centered on the theme of prophecy fulfilled, Luke integrated the theme of prophecy fulfilled with the other themes he deemed important. Luke's recognition of this particular thought is drawn directly by Jesus' own multiple declarations of it.

Luke understood who the potential audience could be, many of them Gentiles. He also understood, by the end of his investigation, how essential the historical context of the Hebrew culture would be to understanding the story he would tell, which is why he carefully explained the Jewish customs, celebrations, and settings throughout the letter. His thoroughness also lent additional credibility to the Jews who received the letter. Luke knew how important it was that the content not only be accurate, but also acceptable to the audience.

Colossians 4:6
Let your conversation be always full of grace, seasoned with salt, so that you may know how to answer everyone.

The apostles themselves, who became Jesus' servants upon His rapture, were blessed to have been eyewitnesses to His ministry. Luke calls them "servants of the Word," recognizing the unique relation of Jesus and the Word (John 1:1-18). It is their stories that had been handed down to-date (at least Mark and the original source known as Q), so Luke had this material available to him as a foundation. However, it is essential to understand that Luke carefully investigated everything. He took time and went to the primary sources of information. Following the formal Greek methodology in the manner in which he is writing, Luke would have performed thorough, empirical research, attempting to get at least two original sources for each story if possible. Think of Luke as an objective journalist, searching to prove his story with irrefutable facts. He wanted to be able to provide Theophilus with a credible testimony. He basically took the position of an apologist in order to prove the case for Christ. To do so for someone like Theophilus makes a lot of sense. Once Theophilus had Luke's manuscript in his hands, he had the means to reproduce and distribute it widely.

Herod the Great ruled Samaria, Galilee, and much of Perea and Coele-Syria from 37-4 BCE. The events in Luke's Gospel took place probably around 6-7 BCE. Abijah was one of the 24 divisions of priests from the family of Aaron, so they served about two weeks every year. Both Zechariah and Elizabeth were from families of priests. The two families most blessed by God throughout the history of the Jews were the priests and the royalty, the family of David. Zechariah and Elizabeth were from the family of Aaron. Later, we will look at two others from the family of David.

"Blameless" does not mean perfect, but it does mean they lived upright lives, attempting to follow God's decrees. Today, we say righteous, having a right relationship with God. The scriptural references the original readers related to would include Noah, Job, and Joseph.

Zechariah and Elizabeth were old, beyond child-bearing age, much like Abraham and Sarah. Luke was setting the stage for a miracle—divine intervention. Zechariah was chosen to serve by lot (Luke 1:9), luck if you will, showing that God can work through all things to accomplish His plan. For Zechariah to serve the priest's duties was a rare opportunity, given the number of other men in his family; they served only twice a year.

The burning of the incense required the priest to go into the Holy of the Holies, the sacred area in which only the serving priest could go. Once Zechariah was secluded behind the veil, an angel appeared to him. Inevitably, the appearance of a divine being to a mortal invoked fear, as it did to Zachariah, but through these appearances, the divine being assured the person not to be afraid. Every time. Luke tells us exactly where the angel was in the room: on the right, the south side of the altar table because the altar faced east. It is this attention to detail that helps illustrate how meticulously Luke researched the facts. He wanted to get everything right, especially when he was telling about an angel from God.

Zechariah was told his prayer would be answered, that his wife would have a son. He was told to name him John (J[eh]ohanan), meaning "The LORD is gracious," or "The LORD has shown favor." The naming rights belonged to the father. In this case, as in Abraham's, God Himself assumed the authority of the father. One of the priest's prayers, as he served the incense, was for God to be gracious to the people, so God's choice of names carried layers of meanings.

Isaiah 30:18
Yet the LORD longs to be gracious to you;
he rises to show you compassion.
For the LORD is a God of justice.
Blessed are all who wait for him!

That John would be a "joy and delight" to Zechariah was obvious. Here was the son he and Elizabeth had been praying for. Many do eventually rejoice, once John's ministry spreads. It had been a long time since Israel had heard from a prophet from God. Zedekiah was the last in 587 BCE. The books of the Inter-Testamentary period speak of the conspicuous absence of the Word of God, but more on that topic later.

John was to be a Nazirite. Samson and Samuel were notable examples of individuals who took this vow to abstain from fermented drink (or any grape product), not to cut his hair, and to avoid dead bodies. The intent, as the Hebrew term implies, was to consecrate, separate, and dedicate a person to God's work and to be holy, in order to perform special work on behalf of God's people.

"And he will be filled with the Holy Spirit." Here Luke introduces for the first time the Holy Spirit, a central theme of the book. Although Luke and Paul agree on most theological basics, the essence of the Holy Spirit differs between the two. Luke's focus clearly leads to the early church's understanding and eventual codification in its creeds of the Trinity. John would be filled with the Holy Spirit, even before his birth.

Psalm 139:13-16
For you created my inmost being;
you knit me together in my mother's womb.

I praise you because I am fearfully and wonderfully made;
your works are wonderful,

I know that full well.

My frame was not hidden from you
when I was made in the secret place,
when I was woven together in the depths of the earth,

Your eyes saw my unformed body.

All the days ordained for me were written in your book
before one of them came to be.

The imagery of John's bringing "many of the people of Israel back to the Lord their God" is straight out of the Hebrew Scriptures and would have been recognized immediately by the first Jewish readers as consistent with earlier prophets who had turned their hearts back to the LORD. The angel continued to foretell John's mission as the one who would prepare the way for the coming of the Lord. First realigning fathers' and children's hearts to each other.

Malachi 4:5-6
See, I will send you the prophet Elijah before that great and dreadful day of the Lord comes. He will turn the hearts of the fathers to their children, and the hearts of the children to their fathers.

John would also turn the disobedient into righteous people, prepared for the arrival of the Lord, all in fulfillment of Isaiah's prophecy:

Isaiah 40:3-5
A voice of one calling:
"In the wilderness prepare
the way for the Lord;
make straight in the desert
a highway for our God.

Every valley shall be raised up,
every mountain and hill made low;
the rough ground shall become level,
the rugged places a plain.

And the glory of the Lord will be revealed,
and all people will see it together.
For the mouth of the Lord has spoken."

Isaiah's reference to "all people" can also be seen as a reference to bringing the Gentiles (disobedient of the Law) into the family of God, thereby fulfilling the prophecy in Proverbs 8 (the Wisdom of Christ).

1 Corinthians 1:30
It is because of him [God] that you are in Christ Jesus, who has become for us wisdom from God.

Thus, John would bring people closer to each other and closer to God,
essentially preparing them for the Greatest Commandment as taught by
Christ, whose way he was preparing.

This deluge of divine information was a lot for Zechariah to take in.
He's still in shock from the presence of the angel. Now he was being told
not only was his wife going to have a son but also his son would be a
prophet in the manner of Elijah. How could this be? He was an old man,
and his wife was beyond child-bearing years. He wanted a sign, some
proof.

The angel gave his credentials, telling Zechariah he was Gabriel ("God
is my hero" or "Mighty man of God"). What was more important, however, was that Gabriel used I AM to tell his name. This was the same I AM
that God used to tell His name to Moses and Jesus used later to clearly
identify His divine status. His position: he stands in the very presence of
God. It was in this presence that Zechariah now stood.

The irony of Zechariah's statement of doubt is obvious. Gabriel was
sent to speak the Good News to him. Because Zechariah did not believe
the angel's words upon hearing words, he would not be able to speak
until they had been fulfilled.

The people were waiting outside for Zechariah to come out and pronounce the Aaronic blessing, so when he could not speak, they quickly
discerned something was amiss. From his gestures, they figured out he
had seen a vision. As a righteous man and priest, Zechariah continued to
complete his duties at the temple until his time was up. Then he and
Elizabeth went home.

When Elizabeth did become pregnant, she stayed secluded in her
home for five months. Why? Because she knew she was carrying a special
child, divinely given, who was to become both a prophet and a Nazirite.
She did not want to jeopardize the sanctity of her child and spent her
time in quiet reflection, prayer, and praise. She declared that God had
blessed her; now she must do her part. After all, she was an elderly,

pregnant woman and needed to take especially good care of herself. The disgrace she mentions is one shared by any woman of that time who was childless. Such a woman was looked down upon. She must have done something wrong that God did not bless her with even one baby! That it is noted for only five months is merely a storytelling feature for Luke, for he quickly moves on and segues to the sixth month in verse 26.

The scene then moves to Nazareth, a town at the northwest corner of Israel, a small town almost in Gentile territory. Most of the action with Zechariah was focused in the Temple in Jerusalem, the center of Jewish life, and then we find Mary in the hinterland. She was a virgin and engaged to Joseph from the house of David. Luke later provides us with Jesus' genealogy in Chapter 3. That she was a descendent of David's fulfilled many of the scripture's prophecies about the lineage of the Messiah. The relationship between Joseph and Mary during this engagement was much stronger than a modern engagement. They were essentially married but not yet living together and could not yet have sexual relations. In Matthew's gospel, he, a Jew, calls them husband and wife. Their relationship could be severed only by a divorce.

Gabriel visited Mary in Nazareth. He immediately acknowledged her as favored, telling her, "The Lord is with you," which foreshadows Immanuel ("God with us"). Mary did not seem to be afraid of the angel; rather, she was troubled at his words. Again, however, the angel said "Do not be afraid." Gabriel then proceeded to tell Mary seven things:

1. She is going to have a child, a son.
2. She is to name him Jesus, Joshua. (English spelling of Yeshua—"God has saved").
3. He will be great.
4. He will be the Son of God.
5. He will have the throne of David.
6. He will reign over the house of Jacob forever.
7. His kingdom will have no end.

Mary was incredulous. She didn't doubt but wondered how she would become pregnant. She hadn't had sex with a man, so how could she have a baby? Gabriel's answer was an insight into both how God works and how Luke sees God working in this gospel story. The Holy Spirit would come over her, and the power of the Most High would overshadow her. The imagery of the latter is similar to that of the power of God hovering over the waters at creation, very powerful.

Exodus 40:35
In the way the Glory of the LORD filled the tabernacle

1 Kings 8:10 & 11
In the way the Glory of God filled the temple

Matthew 17
In the way the Glory of God came in a bright cloud at the Transfiguration

As a result, what would happen would be holy—set aside, dedicated to God for special purposes. Indeed, He would be the Son of God. To illustrate the power of God at work in people, Gabriel pointed to Mary's relative, Elizabeth, who Mary knew was old and past child-bearing years, who was going to have a child and was in her sixth month. "For," Gabriel concludes, "nothing is impossible with God." (Common English Bible–CEB)

Mary's famous answer was one of a servant's heart, humbly and immediately accepting her role, her duty. There was no hesitation, no questions, no arguments, just acceptance. Mary exemplified the attitude Jesus, her son, would teach: that one should first be the servant of others and later be exalted. Having accomplished his task, Gabriel left. Gabriel left, but his presence was gone for only a short time before God's Spirit came to effect Gabriel's prophecy.

Mary wasted no time in getting ready to go see Elizabeth. Mary, young and full of the Holy Spirt, having just conceived Jesus, traveled to the hill country in Judea, probably just west of Jerusalem and Bethlehem. She went to Zechariah's house, entering and calling out to Elizabeth. John leapt in Elizabeth's womb at the sound of Mary's voice, and Elizabeth was filled with the Holy Spirit. God was at work in His people! The inevitable joy that resulted with Mary's appearance gushed out of Elizabeth, blessing Mary above all women and blessing her child. She recognized through the power of the Holy Spirit that Mary's baby would become her Lord. She then confirmed Mary's faithfulness. She believed and was blessed. She was obedient and was blessed, so reminiscent of Abraham:

> Galatians 3:6
> So also Abraham "believed God, and it was credited to him as righteousness."

The power and energy of the Holy Spirit could not be contained. Mary broke out into a song of praise, known as the *Magnificat* because in the Latin Vulgate translation, the first word is *Magnificat*, which means "glorifies." This song is much like Hannah's song (1 Sam 2:1-10), who also benefited from a miracle birth, when all hope was lost and human logic said it was impossible. It is also much like a psalm. Both she and Elizabeth would be familiar with Psalms and Hannah's song, but it was the Holy Spirit that inspired this extemporaneous outpouring of praise.

The song is structured around the theology of a new Israel, while drawing deeply on the Hebrew heritage, so it is founded firmly on the Hebrew Scriptures of the History and the Prophets.

Mary began by glorifying God. Her soul glorified the Lord, and her spirit rejoiced in Him. While much has been made of the difference between the use of soul and spirit in the New Testament, the two are often used interchangeably. Here, as in many of the Psalms, they are used in parallel to reinforce each other. If there is any difference to be made, it could be argued that the soul is the personal essence, which is why in the Common English Bible it is translated as, "With all my heart I glorify the Lord." On the other hand, the spirit is consistently used in the context in relationship between the person and God. What is most important here, however, is Mary's began her song giving God the glory.

The next verse acknowledged her humility and emphasized the theme of God's working with the least likely candidates, the lowly, the disenfranchised to accomplish His plans, such as David, Joseph, and many others. Then she gave credit to God, for it is He who did this miracle for her. From there, she gave a description of God and how He helps the poor and humble and extends mercy to those who venerate Him, as well as Israel from Abraham through his descendants forever.

Mary stayed for three months, taking her to the end of Elizabeth's pregnancy, although Mary is not mentioned in the birth story of John. Also at three months, Mary was into her own second trimester and needed to get home to take care of her own unborn baby.

Luke now turns to the birth of John. Everyone was full of joy for Elizabeth that the Lord had shown her great mercy in her having a child in her old age; and she had a son, just as promised by Gabriel. Being good, law-abiding Jews, Zechariah and Elizabeth circumcised John on the eighth day as prescribed in the Law of Moses.

This was the time to name the child. Because Zechariah still could not talk, their friends and relatives asked Elizabeth if the child should be named after his father, and she obediently replied, per Gabriel's instructions, "He is to be named John." Her response astonished those present, for John was not a family name, so they sought clarification from Zechariah, who confirmed his wife's choice by writing it on a tablet. Zechariah's obedience was rewarded, and he was able to speak again! What did he say? He praised God.

Zechariah's response inspired the neighbors. The testimony of what had happened spread throughout the Judean hill country. All who heard the story were filled with awe. The Lord was obviously at work here, and they wondered what would happen; who would this child become?

Filled by the Holy Spirit, Zechariah burst out in song. This hymn is known as *Benedictus* because the first word in the Latin is "praise be." Zechariah's song is more of a prophecy than Mary's, though it has many of the same references as hers to God's consistent faithfulness toward Israel. As for John, he would be the prophet who prepares the way for the coming of the Lord, helping the people understand their sinfulness and the mercy of God through the forgiveness of their sin, leading to their salvation. The last few lines remind us of Isaiah's prophecy:

Isaiah 9:2
The people walking in darkness
have seen a great light;
on those living in the land of deep darkness
a light has dawned.

Zechariah's song ends with peace. It is the Messiah ("the rising sun") who will bring peace. Indeed, Jesus is the Prince of Peace. It is not peace as the world knows it, the absence of war, but an inward "peace that passes all understanding" (Phil 4:7). This peace is one of the Great Promises of God that **He faithfully promises peace for His people.**

John 14:27
Peace I leave with you; my peace I give you. I do not give to you as the world gives. Do not let your hearts be troubled and do not be afraid.

As John grew up, he grew strong in spirit. The story is written much like Samuel's, who was also a child from a miraculous birth:

1 Samuel 2:26
And the boy Samuel continued to grow in stature and in favor with the Lord and with people.

John matured in the wilderness, a special place in the Jewish culture. It was in the wilderness that they, as a nation, God's chosen people, wandered for forty years. Filled only with wild animals and danger, the desert was a place where nothing good lived. That John came from there indicated two things to the Jews of his day. First, John was not part of the religious establishment centered in Jerusalem. Second, the wilderness often served as imagery of Israel's spiritual emptiness. (John's parents probably died while he was young, in that they were quite old when he was born, so he was probably forced to mature early.)

The desert where John grew up is an area between Jerusalem and the Dead Sea. Although there has been some speculation John grew up with a community of Essenes, John's mission and prophetic approach have little in common with that segregate community. He appeared on the scene when he was about thirty-three years old, as we will see in Chapter Three.

The Wilderness

CHAPTER TWO

L uke continues to identify the timing of events by tying them to historical markers. The enrollment for taxes required each adult over the age of twelve to go to the town of their ancestors. Joseph and Mary were both of the family of David. Because David was born in Bethlehem, they had to travel there to register. Bethlehem means "house of bread." How appropriate the Bread of Life be born there!

There has been much controversy as to what time of year the census took place. Some say at Passover, in the spring. Others have suggested Rome would be more practical and choose the winter so it would not interfere with the economy. An increased burden on the travelers would not have been a Roman concern. The trip from Nazareth to Bethlehem would have taken about three days under good conditions.

Note the economy of words Luke uses in the second chapter, verses 4 through 7. In this short passage, he tells the story of Jesus' birth. No surprise the inn was full, considering all the people streaming into town for the census. Luke is careful to point out that this is Mary's first child. That Mary laid the baby in a manger tells us they stayed with the livestock, which could have been a backroom of the inn or, more likely, a shallow cave next to the inn. It could even have been a temporary tent or make-shift stable put up to accommodate the travelers' animals. We do not know. All we have is the word "manger" in scripture. By this word, we know that Mary and Joseph accepted the most menial accommodations, sleeping with the livestock, and that is where Jesus, the Son of God, was born.

There were always shepherds near Bethlehem. The sheep kept there were regularly purchased and used for temple sacrifices, for the town was on the road most traveled to Jerusalem. These shepherds, guarding the sacrificial lambs, were the first to hear about the birth of the Lamb of God, who would be sacrificed for the sins of the world. We are not told the name of the angel that stood before them but the angel appeared with the glory of the Lord, striking fear into the shepherds. "Fear not," said the angel. The good news was for "all people." Little did these shepherds realize that the salvation brought by the Messiah the angel described, would actually be for everyone for all time. They were given a sign, a distinct sign. How many babies would they expect to find in a manger? The great company of the heavenly hosts appeared suddenly in a flash. These incredible beings that traverse between heaven and earth exploded in praise to God and sang of peace on earth to those whom God favors. Then they vanished.

In their brief, powerful song, the glory was to God. The peace, which Christ would bring (John 14:27), would not be peace as the world had known it. That peace was simply the absence of war, such as the *Pax Romana* that part of the world was experiencing at that time, albeit at the expense of Roman occupation and taxation. Christ's peace would rest on those "whom he favored" (CEB), one of the Great Promises of God. **God faithfully promises peace for His people.**

The shepherds decided they must go see this baby! Even with all the people crammed into the little town of Bethlehem, they found Mary, Joseph, and the baby, just as the angel had told them. They ran through town, telling everyone they met about what has happened. All who heard were amazed.

Mary internalizes all that's happening around her and her child. It had been a long nine months since Gabriel's visit and six months since she left Elizabeth's house. This divine event brought it all back and put the birth into perspective for her as she "committed these things to memory and considered them carefully" (Luke 2:19). Meanwhile, the shepherds, whose lives had been changed forever, returned to their flocks. This time it was they who were glorifying and praising God. They had been instruments in His plan, privileged to have seen first-hand His hand at work in the world.

So why did God choose shepherds? Shepherds were considered scoundrels. They were not ritually clean; they didn't even try to be. If a man couldn't get a job doing anything else, he would often drift out to be a shepherd.

When the shepherds went through town telling this incredible story, how many would believe it, coming from shepherds? Part of Luke's gospel is centered on the presentation of truth (the gospel) and the free-will of the person to accept it or not. This premise is foreshadowed here with the story of Jesus' birth told by the shepherds. It is true, though incredible. Told by those with little credibility, some will choose to believe it and others will not. Later, when John tells of the coming of the Lord, and even later when Jesus' ministry is active, some may remember the shepherds' story and connect the dots. Moses and David were both shepherds when called to lead the nation of Israel. Jesus is later called the Great Shepherd. The paradox of God's using the least expected to perform His work and do great things is juxtaposed against the redeeming quality found in any person at any social strata, a theme that runs throughout the Bible, especially throughout Luke.

Jesus' parents continued to be obedient to God's ways. On the eighth day, he was named and circumcised, meaning they stayed after the census so Jesus could be circumcised in the temple, instead of making the trip home. Although remaining in Bethlehem provided Mary a chance to recover from the birth, it was a sacrifice on their part. Every day they were away from Nazareth was another day Joseph was not making money to support the family.

At the ceremony, Mary and Joseph gave the baby the name as Gabriel had instructed them. On the fortieth day, they take him back to Jerusalem to be presented to the Lord as their first-born. Because they were poor, they gave the sacrifice of the poor: a pair of doves or two young pigeons.

Simeon was one of those known as the "quiet of the land," waiting for the Lord to send a comforter to His people, oppressed by the Romans. He had been told by the Holy Spirit he would see the Messiah before he died. As Mary and Joseph took Jesus in, the Holy Spirit guided Simeon into the temple courts where he would see them and then enabled him to recognize Jesus as the Messiah. What joy this event must have brought to Simeon's heart—finally to see the long-awaited Messiah! His joy overflowed into praise.

Simeon first acknowledged the Lord and then His promise. Simeon confirmed the fulfillment of the promise and saw God's plan for salvation in His Messiah. This plan would include the Gentiles, as prophesied in Isaiah (42:6; 49:6). The praise concluded with the ever-present theme of the Jews of the time: the restoration of the glory of Israel.

Note Simeon's response is the third time Luke illustrated an individual's interaction with the divine resulting in an outpouring of inspired song or praise: Mary, upon Elizabeth's blessing and confirmation, and Zechariah, when John was born and his voice returned. When the Holy Spirit works through willing people to accomplish His work, it inevitably leads to great joy. In the days these events occurred, songs were sung to celebrate such joy, and the Holy Spirit spoke through the songs to glorify God and speak His word.

Although Mary knew what Gabriel had told her, remember, she was just a young girl and probably did not fully comprehend what these prophecies and events meant. Her and Joseph's heads must have been spinning—then Simeon blessed them. Luke does not record the words, but coming from this gentle, old man, full of the Spirit, they were bound to have been gracious and kind. Mary may not have remembered the words so she couldn't tell Luke, but she remembered the prophecy.

Yes, Simeon proceeded to proclaim prophecy. Jesus' teachings would lead some to rise up to be better people, clinging to the truth, while others would find the truth a "stumbling block" (1Cor 1:23). By this claim, their hearts would be revealed. The sword was going to pierce both Jesus and Mary: Him physically, her figuratively.

God was not done. If Simeon's meeting with the promised Messiah was not enough, along came Anna, a prophetess. She was exceptionally old, especially for a widow, who was dependent upon others for sustenance. This woman, who was incredibly devout, first gave glory to God and then proclaimed the truth to anyone who would listen. She acts as a second witness, corroborating Simeon's testimony.

> Deuteronomy 19:15b
> A matter must be established by the testimony of two or three witnesses.

What a day!

The family returned home. Luke is careful to note that Mary and Joseph are obedient to the Law and then stated that as Jesus grew up, He "matured in wisdom and years and in favor with God and with people." This same description was used of Samuel in the same brevity we have of his childhood (1 Samuel 2:26).

Luke does not cover the time in Jesus' childhood when the family went to Egypt to escape Herod's wrath, as Matthew does. The omission is interesting, for that time in Jesus' development would have provided Him with a rich environment for studying His people's history, especially the context of their slavery and eventual salvation by the hand of God. After all, it is He, Jesus, who would provide salvation for all from their slavery to sin.

Suddenly, Jesus was twelve, with Mary and Joseph, going to Jerusalem for the Passover. This trip was no small undertaking. Traveling time was a minimum of six days. Three times a year, a trip was required by the Law: Passover, Festival of Weeks (which later became known as Pentecost), and the Tabernacles. Because they were poor, they could be excused for going to only one, the Passover. All this time they were away from Joseph's work, which was a great personal sacrifice, yet they remained obedient and went every year.

To maintain safety, the families traveled together. After the Passover celebration was completed, the roads were full of pilgrims returning home. It is no wonder Mary and Joseph thought Jesus was with another family for the first day out, for they looked for Him throughout the day. Not finding Him, they immediately returned to Jerusalem and searched for Him for three days. They finally turned to the temple for help and found Him there.

The three-day theme is introduced here. Luke will repeat it again when Jesus tells the Jewish leaders He can tear down the temple and rebuild it in three days, when Jesus says the only sign that will be given this wicked generation will be the sign of Jonah, when the resurrection occurs on the third day. Luke's foreshadowing here is very intentional. This is a critical juncture in Jesus' life when He first publicly exposed himself for who He was (for those with eyes to see). Of course, He knew the scriptures. He is the Word (John 1:14) and more they would find out later, though few if any would remember the brilliant young lad who sat in the temple and amazed them with His answers.

From Luke's description of the exchange going on between Jesus and the teachers, we discover Jesus knows who He is, especially when He responded to his mother's question. Mary, like any caring parent, asked how He could possibly treat His parents this way by not letting them know where He was! But Jesus' answer baffled them. It was not what they expected, yet Jesus, a good son, was obedient to them. Mary continued to cherish these words, as she did when the Magi came. Luke's last sentence here is similar again to the quote from Samuel, only this time it is almost word for word.

Luke 2:52
Jesus matured in wisdom and years, and in favor with God and with people.

1 Samuel 2:26
Meanwhile, the boy Samuel kept growing up and was more and more liked by both the LORD and the people.

CHAPTER THREE

L uke begins this part of his book carefully pinpointing the time with historical references. Using these references, we can ascertain the time to be 26-29 CE. Although Annas had been deposed by the Romans and replaced by Caiaphas, his step-son, the people still held Annas in high regard, and his influence was strong in the ruling hierarchy.

It was during this time that "the word of God came to John," as in the same tradition as many of the previous major prophets.

> 1 Kings 18:1
> After a long time, in the third year, the word of the Lord came to Elijah…

> Jeremiah 1:2
> The word of the Lord came to him in the thirteenth year of the reign of Josiah…

> Ezekiel 1:2-3
> On the fifth of the month—it was the fifth year of the exile of King Jehoiachin— the word of the Lord came to Ezekiel…

The word came to John in the way God speaks to all His prophets, and they must tell it. For what is prophecy if it is not the forth-telling of the Word of God? One is not a prophet unless he is compelled to preach that word. As Paul said in 1 Corinthians 9:16,

"Yet when I preach the gospel, I cannot boast, for I am compelled to preach. Woe to me if I do not preach the gospel!"

John was in the wilderness and would now be about thirty years old. It was at age thirty that a man was considered old enough to become a priest, mature enough to be taken seriously and fit for temple service. John's time had come to serve the Lord who had set him aside from before his birth, indeed before his conception. John went out and called out to the people. He searched for them to bring them God's message. He took the message to where they could easily access him, yet it still required some effort on their part, going out of the town a way to the river. What a great example of evangelism!

John's message was one of the repentance of sins, for which one could be forgiven by confession and baptism. This message was John's commission, which was to prepare the way for Jesus. Luke evoked the prophecy of Isaiah and applied it directly to John. Before a king traveled, the roads were cleared, even leveled and straightened, so Isaiah used this imagery in his prophecy of preparation for the coming of God's savior of the world.

Side note: In Verse 3 the Common English Bible translation, issued 2011, uses "changing their hearts and lives," in lieu of "repentance," which the New International Version (NIV) and other translations use. The CEB updated translation does more accurately reflect, in this author's opinion, the original intent as Luke wrote it and the meaning as inspired by the Holy Spirit.

Luke recognized the work of John as that preparation. This message comes just after Isaiah's famous piece, "Comfort ye my people," and just before "The grass withers and the flowers fall, but the word of our God stands forever." Within the same prophecy, we learn,

Isaiah 40:9-11
You who bring good tidings to Zion,
go up on a high mountain.
You who bring good tidings to Jerusalem,

lift up your voice with a shout,

lift it up, do not be afraid;
say to the towns of Judah,
"Here is your God!"

See, the Sovereign LORD comes with power,
and his arm rules for him.

See, his reward is with him,
and his recompense accompanies him.

He tends his flock like a shepherd:
He gathers the lambs in his arms

and carries them close to his heart;
he gently leads those that have young.

Just like a rabbi, Luke quoted the first part of scripture in order to point the reader/listener to the whole scriptural context from which it came. This method was a very common practice and one which we will see Jesus Himself use later. The verses Luke quoted end with the promise of salvation for all, an early promise of God and a reoccurring theme throughout Luke. This promise is one of the many promises of God found in Luke: one of God's Great Promises.

So, what did this prophet of God say when he was finally unleashed? It wasn't pretty. Rarely is the word of a prophet popular when it is heard. The word of God is harsh when held up against social reality. John did attract crowds. Israel had not seen a real prophet in hundreds of years. Some were there to repent and be baptized, others to support them, others out of curiosity, others for the theater, and others just took in the events and later laughed it off and kept going their own way.

Pharisees also came to see John because so many of the people were there. They needed to see for themselves what all the commotion was about. Was he a real prophet? John spoke directly to them. He didn't speak kindly or respectfully; indeed, he was harsh, unpolished, almost uncivilized. He called them vipers, snakes, symbols of evil, fleeing the fire of judgment, seeking to be spared by ritual baptism, without regard for true repentance of their hearts, much in the same way they followed the letter of the Law while disregarding the spirit of the Law. There was to be no change in their hearts or their lives.

John's exhortation to produce fruit that showed their hearts had changed was consistent with earlier prophets (Isaiah 5), later Jesus' teaching (Luke 6:43&44, 13:6-9; John 15:8), and later the apostles' letters (Colossians 1:10): "Faith without works is dead." If one's heart is truly changed, that person will produce fruit, evidence of the new person he or she has become through repentance. Thus, change in "hearts and life" is the true indicator of repentance.

As for leaning on Abraham as the father of the Jewish nation, the commonly held belief was that God would give special consideration to a Jew simply because of his heritage, that he could trace his ancestry to Abraham. All others, the Gentiles, were "fuel for the fires of hell." John dismissed this argument out-of-hand, saying God could declare anyone to be a child of Abraham.

Having removed their standard crutches, the vulnerable crowd now asked what they should do. John followed with some specific, Christ-like teachings. They were Christ-like, in that they reinterpreted the Law in such a way that was new and fresh, yet consistent with the intent of the original covenant. These teachings opened their eyes and made them wonder if John was the long-awaited Messiah.

John's reply shows us he knew his role in history: to prepare the way for the Messiah. He humbly positioned himself as a lowly servant and Christ as the coming judge. Christ will separate the righteous and unrepentant, regardless whether they are Jewish or not.

John's abrasive manner did not stop with the Pharisees. Herod Antipas divorced his first wife in order to marry his niece, Herodias, who had been married to his brother. This disgraceful arrangement was morally wrong and against the Law. John spoke out openly and directly to Herod about his marriage and other evil deeds he had done. There was no shortage of the latter. Herod being a paranoid, manipulative leader, killing those whom he suspected of threatening him in any way. Apparently, John spoke too loudly once too often, and Herod had him locked away in prison.

Before John's imprisonment, however, Jesus came to him to be baptized. Luke's account of the occasion is unusually abbreviated but included three important facts. First, Jesus was praying during this very public symbolic act. Luke continues to point out Jesus' praying and how often he prayed throughout the book, thereby relaying how important prayer was to Jesus. Second, the Holy Spirit came to Jesus in a bodily form, a visible sign to all. Third, God spoke words of confirmation, which echoed the voice of prophecy:

Isaiah 42:1
Here is my servant, whom I uphold,
my chosen one in whom I delight;
I will put my Spirit on him,
and he will bring justice to the nations.

It is in this scene that we see, for the first time since Jesus' birth, the Holy Trinity together. Jesus' baptism marked the beginning of His public ministry, complete with the fulfillment of prophecy, as well as the presence of the Triune God. Luke set Jesus' age around thirty, which aligns with John's and the historical timeline he established earlier.

Luke then outlines a genealogy for Jesus. These were very important to Jews. The Jews could trace their ancestry back to Abraham. If they could not, they would not be considered truly Jewish. Luke went further and traced Jesus' lineage back to Adam, the first man, emphasizing the universal role of the savior. His genealogy from David to Joseph actually traced Mary's side of the family, the bloodline, for Joseph was not Jesus' physical father, and Mary was a descendant of David.

CHAPTER FOUR

J esus left the Jordan River where He was baptized, "full of the Holy Spirit." The Spirit led Him into the wilderness. At that time, the wilderness was dangerous. Many wild animals lived there. Mark's gospel states, "He was with the wild animals, and angels attended him" (1:13). Mark's gospel, being the earliest one published, would have been available to Luke while he was researching his book, and he certainly got most of his information from those with whom Jesus had walked, those who had heard the story from His own lips. This wilderness is the same one from which John came, having been prepared by God for his mission there. Yes, one of God's Great Promises: **He faithfully prepares his people.** Now, He would help prepare His son for His mission.

Jesus was not truly alone during His forty days in the desert. The Spirit was with him, along with God's angels protecting Him, yet He did not eat during this time. The forty days is reminiscent of the forty years Israel wandered in the desert until they had been purged and prepared to enter the Promised Land. They also remind us of the forty days Moses spent (twice) alone with God on the mountain receiving the Law (Exodus 24:18, 34:28) and like Elijah (1 Kings 19:8). This was a holy time of fasting and prayerful communion when Jesus, the man, was fully prepared to perform His mission to change humanity.

The scripture tells us Satan tested Jesus during all this time. Apparently, Jesus resisted Satan's testing through the forty days. At the end of that time, He was famished, both from the time and the energy it took to fight Satan. Satan's first recorded test appealed to that hunger because Satan always strikes at one's weakest point.

In the desert, there were rocks that resemble loaves of bread littering the ground. How easy to deceive a starving man into seeing these as bread! How easy it would have been for Jesus to have changed just one of them into bread to satisfy his hunger. There were no witnesses, but the truth of one's character is revealed when one is alone and faced with a difficult, tempting choice. Note Satan's wording as well. "If you are the Son of God..." Yes, He is. How easy it would be for him to prove it too. Satan's temptation is much like the original temptation of Adam—to ply doubt into God's provision and provide for yourself. "Don't just let the angels help, do it yourself. You are the Son of God, right?"

Jesus, the one who would become the Bread of Life, understood all things, answered. He, who is the Word made flesh, rebutted Satan with scripture. "One's life does not depend on the food eaten but is sustained by God." We're talking about life here, not just food. And Christ knew all about life. He was there when it was created.

> Deuteronomy 8:3
> He humbled you, causing you to hunger and then feeding you with manna, which neither you nor your fathers had known, to teach you that man does not live on bread alone but on every word that comes from the mouth of the LORD.

Satan's second recorded temptation was based on lies, for he did not have all the authority over the world or the power to give any of it to anyone. Yet this temptation was strong, in that it would be a short-cut to glory, bypassing the torture and the cross. Jesus not only knew He must suffer and die in order for God's plan to be fulfilled, but He also knew God alone is to be worshiped.

> Deuteronomy 6:13
> Fear the LORD your God, serve him only.

The third recorded temptation took place in God's chosen city, Jerusalem. Satan then enlisted scripture for his purpose (which he still does). While it is true God would have protected Jesus from harm had He thrown Himself from the top of the temple in view of the crowds, this dramatic miracle would have had a short life-cycle and accomplished little toward the goal of salvation.

Deuteronomy 6:16
Do not test the LORD your God.

While we admire Jesus for His resistance to Satan's temptations and the manner in which He did it, it is important to note Satan's reaction was simply to leave and wait for another opportunity. Temptations, even though conquered, even though defeated by the Word of God, can and will reappear again when least expected and at our most vulnerable times. It happened to the Son of God; it will happen to us.

Jesus, in full communion with the Father and charged with the Holy Spirit, finished His journey home to Galilee. He taught in the synagogues. It appears He taught there for quite a while, maybe as long as a year, based on what we gather from the other gospels, especially John.

Jesus went to His home synagogue, "as he normally did." By standing, He volunteered to read scripture. It was His intent to announce publicly the nature of His ministry to those of His hometown. We don't know why the attendant gave Him the scroll of Isaiah. Was that the one from which they were currently reading? Regardless of the reason, it was the book from which Jesus wanted to read the passage He read. He found the passage in Isaiah that spoke directly to the Messiah's mission. Note that in the first line, with Jesus Himself reading it, we have again the Holy Trinity present. He sat down, which was the proper position for teaching, and bluntly declared that the scripture had been fulfilled immediately when they heard it read.

The people tried to reconcile this bold declaration of Jesus being God's son and their own understanding of Jesus as "Joseph's son."

They had heard of Jesus performing miracles in Capernaum and were probably thinking, "If He would perform miracles here like he did there, we might believe Him." Knowing their petty thoughts, Jesus not only cut them off but also confronted them with the truth that if He were rejected by the Jews, as were Elijah and Elisha, then salvation would be extended to Gentiles, just as their ministries were. These words tipped the scales. No longer could they tolerate Him in their presence. He had violated a sacred truth of the Jewish tradition: only Jews would be saved by God. They drove Jesus to a cliff at the edge of town in order to throw Him off, but He passed through the crowd and went on His way. Luke doesn't tell the reader how Jesus accomplished His exit.

Jesus left Nazareth and returned to Capernaum, a major city on the north end of the Sea of Galilee. It was the home of Peter, Andrew, and others, a hub of Jesus' early ministry. He taught on the Sabbath because the people were all working the other six days of the week. His teaching was received differently by the people. He taught with authority. What they were used to was hearing the Scribes say, "There is a saying that..." or "Rabbi so-and-so said..." always referring to an authority to back up what they were teaching. Jesus, on the other hand, was direct, saying to them, "I say to you..." When a speaker has authority, it becomes readily apparent to the audience, all the more so on the spiritual level. The Holy Spirit will work through the speaker and the listener, both to clarify what is being said to the individual listener and to convict the listener of the truth of what is being said. No wonder the people were "amazed at his teaching."

At the synagogue, Jesus was confronted by evil. A man was possessed by a demon. Luke is careful to point out this demon was an evil spirit, one which could cause physical or mental illness, violence, or other socially unacceptable behavior. The spirit recognized Jesus for who He was. From the spiritual world, this evil being saw Jesus' spiritual identity and correctly identified Him.

In response, Jesus gave two commands. First, He stifled the demon, "Silence!" Then He exorcised him from the man, "Come out of him!" The results are immediate and complete. The people were again amazed. The exorcisms they had seen performed before were elaborate affairs, with lengthy, complicated rituals (justifying their cost no doubt). This man from Nazareth simply spoke, and the demons obeyed! The people were "shaken," as are all mortals when confronted with the divine.

So word spread about Jesus. He taught with authority, not like anyone else, and He cast out demons with a word, such authority He had. This man was someone special.

Jesus went to Simon's house. He knew Simon from previous trips to Capernaum. Simon was married, and his mother-in-law was ill. They asked Jesus to help her. (All three synoptic gospels tell this story but only Luke, the physician, adds the detail that she was suffering a high fever.) Jesus simply rebuked the fever, and the fever left her. His words to the fever were harsh. The Word of God goes out to accomplish His will. Often it is gentle; sometimes "normal" or hidden, unrecognizable; and other times harsh, all depending on what is necessary.

Because it was the Sabbath, the people were restricted on how much they could carry and how far, including their sick loved ones. That evening, as the sun set, marking the end of the Sabbath, the people had heard of Jesus' healing the man with the demon, so they brought to Simon's house friends and relatives with all kinds of illnesses and demon possession. Note, this story was not a story of mass healing. Luke was careful to point out that Jesus laid His hands on "each one." None was turned away. All were healed. Demons tried to expose Jesus for who He was, but He silenced them because it was not yet time for the people to know who He really was.

Jesus almost always silenced those who wanted to expose His divinity, even up to Peter's declaration. He did not want the prevailing, false image of Messiah hung on Him. No, the real and complete picture would not be clear until after the resurrection. Only then would the people, even His disciples, begin to understand who God's Messiah was.

Though He must have worked late into the night, at the break of day, Jesus went out to a deserted location to pray. The people selfishly wanted Him to stay in Capernaum. They wanted this fascinating, powerful teacher and healer to stay in their town, but Jesus told them He must fulfill His mission to preach the good news of the kingdom of God to other towns. Ah, the Kingdom of God! This is Luke's introduction of the term, which he applies in different ways through his book. Appropriately, here Luke first mentions it in a general sense. From Capernaum, Jesus goes and teaches throughout Judea.

CHAPTER FIVE

J esus returned to Capernaum, His ministry's home base. The people
found out He was back in town and crowded around Him by the
edge of the sea to hear His teaching about the word of God. With all
the people pushing each other to get close, it was hard for Jesus to get in
a position where everyone could see and hear Him. Jesus saw a couple of
boats that had come in from fishing all night, He chose Simon's and asked
him to push out just a little to give Him an ideal spot from which He
could address the crowd.

After He had finished teaching, He told Simon to put out into deep
water and let down his nets. That would be pretty far out. The shallows
there run at least one hundred yards, and here is this carpenter/preacher
telling a very tired fisherman what to do. Simon objected; what Jesus
wanted him to do didn't make any sense. You fished in the depths at
night and in the shallows during the day. They had fished hard all night
and caught nothing, yet Jesus wanted them to go back to the deep water.
Really? But so strong is the hold Jesus already had on Simon that he
would obey simply because He asked.

The result was nothing short of miraculous. The catch was more than
Simon could handle. He got his partners with the other boat to come
help, but there were so many fish they couldn't manage them all without
risking sinking both boats. This catch was overwhelming.

Simon was overcome. The scene suddenly changed from a crowd on
the shore watching to just Simon and Jesus, intimately personal. Simon
realized he was in the presence of the divine, which forced him to
confront himself with his own sinfulness. Oh, what fear divine revelation

can drive into a person's heart! How many times do we see this in history where people were faced with the divine only to see just how unclean they were? Abraham, Job, Isaiah, Moses and so many of the prophets. Apparently James and John were just as amazed and awestruck, but Simon (Luke adds Peter just to clarify) spoke first, as he often did. Of course, from God's own heart came the words of reassurance, "Do not be afraid," followed by the famous call to Simon, John, and James, the first disciples, to become fishers of men. They left everything to follow Jesus.

This radical discipleship may shock our modern sensibilities somewhat. Grown, responsible men leaving their families to follow a rabbi? Their decision was not totally uncommon though, especially when the rabbi exhibited true prophetic character. The remnant of tradition of the supremacy of the Word of God still held sway in the culture that allowed a man and his family to sacrifice their normal lives for the pursuit of truth, for indeed, they all served God. Jesus offered that pursuit and more. Later, he would substantiate Peter's questioning about abandoning their every-day lives for Him and explain the rewards they would receive for their faithfulness. Here, Jesus had generously provided their families with a bounteous catch of fish, the sale of which would help sustain them for a long time.

Luke introduces the healing of the leper here at this juncture of Jesus' ministry. The leper, in lieu of keeping his prescribed distance, put social restrictions aside and directly approached Jesus, posturing in the manner of worship with his face to the ground. From where did the leper's faith come? How did he know Jesus? We don't know, but apparently he had complete faith in His ability to cure him of this tenacious disease that prevented him from participating in society and worshiping God in his synagogue.

Jesus simply touched the man and healed him. To touch a leper was socially forbidden and against the Law. The common understanding was that leprosy was highly contagious and communicable by touch. Jesus' disciples were probably shocked at the sight of Jesus touching the leper, yet when they saw the resultant healing, they learned (again) that they were not with just any ordinary man, and the rules did not apply to Him. The healing and mercy that flowed from Jesus were far stronger than any disease or demon He would encounter. Luke intentionally puts this story early in his gospel, when the first disciples had just joined with Jesus, to illustrate how radical this ministry would be in which they would be participants.

Jesus' directions to the healed man were straight out of the Hebrew Scripture: be humble, do not tell anyone, but go and report to the priest and offer the sacrifices required by the Law. But such miracles did not go by unnoticed. News spread, and there was much sickness among the people, so they sought out this man who could heal. Here Luke bluntly states that even with this demand, Jesus often went away to pray. The balance between the demands on Jesus' power and His need to pray is quickly established and will be reinforced throughout Luke's story.

Luke now brings onto the stage the beginning of conflict between Jesus and the established church of the day. The Pharisees represented the educated, the "separated ones," who had put aside the world to dedicate themselves to the scripture. They interpreted scripture for the people, taught in the synagogues, and considered the regulations (case law) to be as important as the Law of Moses because they were applicable and understandable. These rules had been developed over hundreds of years, and every single rule had a good reason for its existence. The regulations were for the good of the people, founded in God's Law, extrapolated to their everyday existence.

Most Pharisees were good men, striving to live the Law, obeying every commandment to the letter. Unfortunately, as it is with any group that achieves a role of power in society, many became corrupted by this power and took advantage of their position. Some rules then became reinforcement of the status-quo to maintain that power, position, and prestige. Anything that threatened the stability of the status-quo was highly suspect and intently scrutinized. These Pharisees and their Scribes, the actual teachers of the Law, traveled from all over the surrounding area to investigate this itinerant preacher, who was making quite a name for Himself by what He was doing, saying, and the apparent authority by which He was acting. Not only were the Pharisees and Scribes where Jesus is teaching, but also the crowd is quite large.

Then, Luke specifically points out that "the power of the Lord" was with Jesus to heal. This theme of Jesus' power runs through Luke. It appears to be a subtle introduction to the mysterious integration of the Holy Trinity. We have already seen a couple of glimpses of the Holy Trinity, and now Luke, almost casually, mentions that Jesus, the Son of God, has power from God to heal. The only surprising thing is that Luke, with his focus on the Holy Spirit, did not mention the Holy Spirit by name.

To this crowd came some men with their paralytic friend. They want to see him healed too, but they couldn't get through the crowd. Rather than give up, they climbed up on top of the roof of the building, removed some of the tiles, and lowered their friend's mat down right in front of Jesus and the others present. They persevered. They knew if they could only get their friend in front of Jesus, he could be healed. Their faith was rewarded. Because of their faith, their friend was healed.

Jesus, however, did not tell the paralytic, "You are healed, stand up and walk." Instead, He said, "Friend, your sins are forgiven." Given the context, with the Pharisees and Scribes in attendance, Jesus intentionally used this tact. It got the expected reaction: the religious leaders immediately began to think Jesus had committed blasphemy, for only God had the power to forgive sins. Blasphemy was considered the greatest sin a person could commit, and here Jesus had committed it right in front of them! Of course, He knew what they were thinking.

It was time to confront them with the truth, in front of many witnesses about who He was and what power He had. "Why do you fill your minds with questions?" Doubts, wonders, and fears. Which is easier? Both statements are equally easy for the Son of God to say; both will yield the same result for Him. All things are possible for God. To show them and all the others in attendance, that He, Jesus, was in fact the Son of God and had the authority to heal and forgive sins, He tells the man, "Get up, take up your cot, and go home." Luke records how the man praised God for his healing, and the people were filled with awe and glorified God. No note of the Pharisees' or Scribes' reactions is given.

Jesus' self-designated term for himself, Son of Man, is worth examination. Although the Common English Bible, the most recent modern

English translation, has chosen to use "Human One," Son of Man is still more familiar and resonates better with its original meaning. Jesus, knowing all scripture, history, context and meaning, took this title from Hebrew Scripture. It is used there only a couple of times, some to illustrate people's humanity and to reinforce humility, such as with Ezekiel. In Daniel's prophecy, He alludes to one who will be used by God for judgment on the earth and again in a similar way later in The Revelation to John. Although Jesus is God Immanuel, He is fully human and takes on all the frailty of being a man. He totally identifies with those with whom He lives and those He sees suffering.

After healing many, Jesus left the house and saw Levi, a tax collector at his booth. Tax collectors were Jews who had formed an alliance with the Romans to collect their taxes for Rome. They profited well from this trade. Most were corrupt, in that the more they collected, the more they kept for themselves. The other Jews hated them, taking them for traitors, and they were perpetually unclean and unable to participate in the synagogue or temple because they were breaking the Law by the very nature of what they were doing. Tax collectors were the most hated members of the community.

Levi surely knew who Jesus was. He knew who everyone was, yet when Jesus walked up to him this day and told him to follow Him, he left everything and followed Jesus. Then Levi (who later became known as Matthew) celebrated the way tax collectors do: he threw a big party and invited his fellow tax collectors and associates. The Pharisees and Scribes were shocked and offended. They complained to Jesus' disciples about His associating with such scum.

Jesus' response was classic. He told them He had come to minister to the sick, not the healthy. Were there any folk ready to stand up and declare themselves healthy and in no need of this physician? They had seen the miracle healings He had done. Could they really believe they didn't need healing themselves? Luke again records no reaction. The time has not yet come for Jesus' plan.

The Pharisees and Scribes did, however, have more questions. They didn't understand why Jesus' disciples didn't fast and pray like the disciples of the Pharisees and even John the Baptist. Jesus offered them a veiled prophecy. While some of the more astute students of the scripture may have understood Him, His reference to the bridegroom probably left most of them in the dark. He was referring to Himself and suggesting that, once He was gone, His disciples would then fast as other disciples. This reference is also a subtle foreshadowing of Christ as the bridegroom and the church as the bride, as related in eschatological literature.

Then Jesus went one step more and gave them a parable to ponder. The essence is that for new wine, the winemaker must use new wine skins. Similarly, for a new gospel, disciples must use a new paradigm. Many people, however, are just fine and comfortable with the old.

CHAPTER SIX

‹›

T he Sabbath was holy to the Jews and keeping it holy was one of the Ten Commandments, the foundation of all the Law. The Sabbath has always been integral with God's plan for life, even part of creation itself. Unfortunately, over the years, the Scribes' interpretations of how this vital law should be applied to everyday life became a complex web of trivial rules. The focus then, as with many (or most) of the laws, became how to keep up with the rules under so many circumstances and not on the original intent of the law. The Sabbath ran from sundown Friday until sundown Saturday.

On one Sabbath, Jesus' disciples plucked a few heads of grain, rubbed them in their hands to shuck them, and had a little snack. Some Pharisees, who were obviously watching Jesus and His disciples to see what they might do wrong, saw this act as a violation of Sabbath law. They were harvesting! Jesus reminded them of when David, revered by all Jews, asked for and received the bread of the presence from the priests for himself and his men when he was being pursued and was famished. The bread was, by law, for the priests only, but the priest gave David the bread out of compassion (1Samuel 21:1-6).

Jesus followed with a bold statement: "The Son of Man is Lord of the Sabbath." Luke once more does not give us the Pharisees' reactions, but they must have been astounded. Such a declaration would have been clear blasphemy in their minds.

Luke, the storyteller, takes us to another scene on another Sabbath, where Jesus was being tested by the Pharisees. The stage was set. There was a crowd in the synagogue. A man with his right hand withered was there. (Note the attention to detail Luke gives by stating which hand was withered.) The Pharisees and teachers of the Law lay in wait. Jesus understood perfectly and took full advantage of the situation. He called the man to the front, and then, as He often did, Jesus asked a question they didn't expect. In this case, they did not answer. They didn't dare. Either answer would be wrong. So when the man's hand was restored, they were furious. At themselves? At Jesus? Because their setup was foiled? Obviously, there was no rejoicing in the man's healing. This time, Luke gives us our first peek at the Pharisees' intentions. They began to plot what they might do to Jesus.

Jesus now prepared to make one of the most important decisions of His ministry. Just how important the selection of the twelve apostles is becomes apparent later when the church is beginning to form. These men, minus Judas Iscariot, were fully human, yet they stood up to incredible pressures to spread the gospel, sustain the early church, and provide some of the written scripture that becomes part of what we know today as the Bible. They were to be his apostles, representatives, specially appointed to speak for him, commissioned.

Jesus selected these twelve men after spending the night in prayer on the side of a mountain, alone with God.

Luke's version of this sermon is shorter than Matthew's. Jesus no doubt gave the same sermon several times in different places, and certainly it varied somewhat from place to place. Luke chose the points most important to him and to those from whom he gathered his information. There are parts of Matthew's version that can be found in other parts of Luke.

There was a great crowd at the base of the mountain. Many disciples and others traveled a long way to see Jesus, the man who could heal their diseases. Jesus did not disappoint them, including curing those with evil spirits. Jesus' sermon came across as counter-intuitive, but the main point was to establish a value system in which one shared blessings with those less fortunate, and the privileged no longer exploited the disenfranchised. The sufferings in this life are temporary and not to be compared with the blessings to be found in eternal life.

The blessings (using the older translations) are all promises, some of **God's Great Promises**. These are simply stated, easy to understand, and comforting to those who lack such things in this world now.

If people are persecuted for their belief in Christ, then they should rejoice, for their reward will be great in heaven. This statement came back to the apostles when the early church suffered persecution within its first year and under Saul of Tarsus.

The woes strike hard (Luke 6:24-26) at those who are comfortable and complacent in their prosperity, who ignore those in need, and those who don't think they need God, only themselves and their own individual effort. Jesus lays these woes out point-for-point as negative counterparts of the blessings.

Luke then continues to share some of Jesus' core teachings.

Love was at the center of Jesus' teachings. The love he taught went beyond what the people had learned from the teachers of the Law and far beyond the parochial applications, which led them to understand that they were the Chosen People whom God favored. Jesus taught unconditional love toward everyone, even one's enemies. Although the Golden Rule had been taught by others earlier, Jesus reframed it in a positive statement and made it universally applicable. To hold ourselves up to God's standard of mercy and compassion is indeed a challenge from Jesus.

Jesus continued by teaching about fairness: the way we treat others will determine how we are treated. He warned us not to be hypocritical. What we say and do is indicative of what is in our hearts.

> Psalm 51:10-12
> Create in me a pure heart, O God,
> and renew a steadfast spirit within me.
>
> Do not cast me from your presence
> or take your Holy Spirit from me.
>
> Restore to me the joy of your salvation
> and grant me a willing spirit, to sustain me.

One who hears Christ and puts His words in practice will be able to withstand the forces of this world; the one who does not will be swept away by them. In other words, the ultimate hypocrisy is hearing the truth and not acting on it. Obedience is key when hearing the Word of God. As Jesus states in John 14:23,

"Anyone who loves me will obey my teaching."

Luke firmly believed in this principle. When a person is faced with the truth of Christ, he must inevitably make a life decision and, thereby, determine his fate.

CHAPTER SEVEN

L uke's segue into the next scene is interesting, and most take no notice of his carefully constructed phrasing. The CEB captures it best, with the imagery of Jesus sowing his words among the people.

Luke 7:1a
After Jesus finished presenting all his words among the people…

The clear implication is that some of these seeds sown will take root and grow, making for future disciples when the church forms later. Others may take the lessons and simply live a better life. There are always those who will take what they choose and dismiss the rest or even dismiss it all, much like Jesus' parable of the seed.

Jesus went back into town, Capernaum and was met with some of the elders of the town asking him to help a Roman centurion. Though the term used to mean, as the name implies, the leader of 100 men, it had changed over the years and could mean an army officer over a certain territory with authority about 80 soldiers. Regardless, the standards for the rank were high. Character, leadership, and loyalty were as important as military successes. That the locals admired him for loving their nation meant that he had studied the culture enough to appreciate it fully and forged a bond with the people, even to the extent of building them a synagogue. Jesus readily understood why the elders thought this man deserved some attention and may have already known who he was, having spent a considerable amount of time in Capernaum.

The centurion's servant was so ill he was about to die. He was very important to the centurion who obviously cared about him by seeking Jesus' help to make him well. He got word that Jesus was on His way to his house and sent some friends to dissuade Him. A visit was not necessary. He did not even feel he was worthy to come and meet Jesus himself —he didn't deserve such an honor. Jesus needed only to say the word for the healing to happen. (The term Luke uses is "completely cured," a medical term, something we might expect from the physician.) The centurion understood authority and clearly understood Jesus' authority. Jesus, however, made the occasion a teaching moment for all those crowded around to make two points clear. First, faith without sight was greater than faith after seeing. Second, God's blessings were not limited to the Jews but were given to those who ask.

The humility of the centurion cannot go without recognition. He is undoubtedly a powerful man, yet he did not demand Jesus come into his home. Indeed, he humbly declined, declaring himself to be unworthy. Those that humble themselves shall be exalted.

Luke takes us to another scene of Jesus' local ministry, the town of Nain, about 12 miles as the crow flies—maybe a day's walk. When He and His disciples approached the town, a funeral parade was going out, carrying the only son of a single mother, now a widow. Widows were the most disenfranchised people in society. They had no means of income, no man to provide for them. As women, they were already less than a second-class citizen. It is no wonder that God, through His prophets, spoke out for the "widows and the orphans," the weakest of society.

Jesus saw the woman's plight and had compassion for her. "Don't cry," He said. "Don't be afraid." When He touched the coffin, those carrying it stopped. They were shocked. No one came near a dead body because it would make them unclean. They sacrificed purity for their friend to bury her son. But Jesus stopped them. He had authority in His actions. "Proceed no closer to the grave!" He told them. The coffin would have been open on top so all could see the body. Jesus spoke to the man telling him to get up, and the widow's son sat up and talked. A simple word and the man lived again. The power of the word of God!

Isaiah 55:11

**"so shall my word be that goes out from my mouth;
it shall not return to me empty,**

**but it shall accomplish that which I purpose,
and succeed in the thing for which I sent it..."**

The power of God's Word is manifested in Christ. His words spoken to the young man were words of life. His words gave the dead man life.

Jesus then gave him back to his mother. What joy she must have felt! The people praised God. They recognized the power was from Him, so Jesus must have been a prophet, ordained by God sent to help God's people. Of course, this story spread quickly throughout the territory. The term "Great Prophet" rolled off the people's tongues, referring to Elisha, who raised the Shunammite widow's only son from death (2Kings 4, not far from Nain). "To help his people" was the beginning of the people's refrain, drawing from the Messianic prophecies, such as Isaiah's.

But they did not know what they were saying. What is a prophet but one who speaks forth the word of God? Sometimes, it tells of future events, but more often it tells of the current state of the people's hearts and their distance from God. Read the prophets and you will read what was on God's heart about His people. Jesus is the Word, the incarnation of God; He is the ultimate prophet. Little did the people of his day understand what they were saying when they said a "Great Prophet" was among them.

While Jesus' ministry had grown from telling the good news, healing the sick, casting out demons, saving those about to die, and even raising the dead, his cousin John sat in Herod's jail. Alone except for occasional communications with his own disciples, John hears about Jesus. He did not hear some of the things he expected. There was no talk of God's army overthrowing the Romans, establishing His rule on earth, and making Jerusalem His capital. The Messiah he knew from scripture had not manifesting himself the way John had anticipated. Yes, he would be the Lamb of God, but he was also supposed to triumph over his foes. Confused and alone in his cell, over time, John began to wonder, so he asked two of his trusted friends to go to Jesus and ask him directly if He was the Messiah.

Jesus' response was to show the friends in ascending order of magnitude what He had been doing. All of these miracles were prophesied in Isaiah, and John would readily recognize who He was and understand His acts as those of the Messiah.

Isaiah 29:18
In that day the deaf will hear the words of the scroll,
and out of gloom and darkness
the eyes of the blind will see.

Isaiah 35:5–6a
Then will the eyes of the blind be opened
and the ears of the deaf unstopped.

Then will the lame leap like a deer,
and the mute tongue shout for joy.

Isaiah 61:1
The Spirit of the Sovereign LORD is on me,
because the LORD has anointed me
to preach good news to the poor...

Jesus ends with a word of encouragement for John; he is not to doubt or be discouraged.

Jesus then talked to the crowd about John. They all knew who he was. Jesus reminded them that they didn't go see him because he was a showman, dressed up with fancy words. No, they went to see him because he was a prophet. Then Jesus quoted Malachi 3:1, which refers to the second coming of Elijah. Luke 6:28 is an incredible double statement. First Jesus said that John was the greatest person who ever lived. Then, He quickly stated that the least in the Kingdom of Heaven is greater than John! This is one of those paradoxes Jesus tossed out that makes our heads spin, but He continuously reinforced His message of the primacy of the Kingdom of God.

Luke then puts his own spin on Jesus' message with a parenthetical paragraph. Those who had been baptized by John agreed with what Jesus said; those that had not, did not. According to Luke, the Pharisees and experts in the law "rejected God's will for their lives" by not being baptized by John when they had a chance. They were confronted by the truth and chose not to accept it. Luke viewed this decision as rejecting God's will for them: that they be saved.

Jesus tried to put His comments into perspective, both for His disciples and for the Pharisees and Scribes. He compared the Jews of the day to children. That alone is a derogatory approach, for children were considered the least of society. He said they didn't respond to either fun music or a funeral dirge, throwing two extremes at them to illustrate their callousness. He further elaborated by showing them John's (the Baptist) ministry, which was based on strict adherence to the Law and repentance with Jesus' ministry and which they saw as frivolous and cavalier. The summary, however, was that "wisdom is proved right by all her children." Jesus offered "wisdom" here as a periphrasis for the name of God. Both His and John's ministries may have appeared quite different to the Pharisees and scribes, but their source and their goal were one and the same, and a wise person could see that. God's wisdom, then, is proven right by His children who choose His Son.

A Pharisee, Simon, invited Jesus to his house for dinner. Most certainly his invitation was to ply Him with questions, hoping to trip Him up or expose Him in some way. Jesus accepted and reclined at the table, which was the usual posture for eating at the time–lying on one's left elbow and eating with the right hand with the feet stretched out behind.

That a woman entered the house while they were eating was not that surprising. The houses were generally open with a courtyard leading into a large room, which is probably where the dinner was being served. This particular woman was a prostitute. She was weeping. Not just crying but bawling, gushing—the kind of behavior that was truly embarrassing. She had her hair down, something women simply did not do, except in front of their husband, but, of course, she had no husband. She anointed Jesus' feet. She really couldn't get to His head, but His feet were right where she could access them, so she washed them with her tears. She performed the task of the lowest slave: washing the feet of a guest. She then anointed them with her perfume. The phial is the type Jewish women wore around their neck and was shaped like a tear-drop and fit between their breasts. It was very expensive, usually taking about a year's wages to pay for. It was intended to anoint their husband's head on their wedding night. This woman was sacrificing her personal fortune in a totally uninhibited manner without regard to anyone else in the world. No doubt, she had heard Jesus preach, repented of her sinful life, and wanted to show her extreme gratitude for God's mercy. She had indeed a change in heart and wanted to start a new life.

All the theatrics were a little too much for Simon. If Jesus were really a prophet, He would know the woman was a prostitute without even having to turn around. How dare He allow this to go on in his house in front of his friends! While he was still in shock, searching for the right thing to say, Jesus says he has something to tell him.

Jesus spoke of two men who owed money. The CEB translation puts the story into perspective well.

> Luke 7:41b
> "One owed enough money to pay five hundred people for a day's work. The other owed enough money for fifty."

Based on an average income of $50,000 per year, the first debtor would owe about $69,000; the other about $690. Neither debtor could repay his debt. The moneylender canceled both debts. Which would love him more? Simon answered somewhat hesitantly. He was afraid it was a trick question but gave the only obvious answer. Jesus affirmed Simon's answer, and Simon felt pretty good about being right in front of his guests.

Now Jesus turned back to the woman. Simon started getting uncomfortable. Jesus laid out the facts. He came to Simon's house as requested, but Simon did not offer Jesus any water with which to wash His feet. The woman, on the other hand, cleaned His feet with her tears and dried them with her hair–an extraordinary act above and beyond common hospitality. Simon offered Jesus no kiss of greeting, normally done for guests, nor had His feet washed. The woman, however, has been continuously kissing His feet and poured perfume on them. These acts by her were evidence of her uninhibited love, expressed from her thankfulness. Because of her repentance, her sins were forgiven. She knew Jesus would forgive her, and she wanted to give everything she had in thankfulness. Jesus rewarded her faith and granted her peace. He left the guests to wonder who this man was that forgives sins.

CHAPTER EIGHT

J esus' ministry then changes in focus from being centered in Caperna-
    um to more of a mobile ministry, moving from town to town
throughout Galilee. With Him were the core twelve apostles and some
women. Luke is careful to point out the women, more than the other
gospel writers, and their important role. Many of them financially supported the mission. Others were there out of gratitude for being healed.
Mary Magdalene had seven demons removed, seven being the number of
completeness, indicating she had been completely possessed. Mary was a
very common name then, and she is not to be confused with the sinful
woman of Chapter Seven or other women named Mary, such as Mary of
Bethany or Mary, the mother of James and John.

Apparently, there were many women who helped support the mission
but they did not travel with them. One was Joanna, probably the wife of
Cuza, the manager of Herod's household. The manager was a highly
entrusted and well compensated position; therefore, Joanna would have
had access to wealth.

Jesus was "preaching and proclaiming the good news of God's kingdom."
Luke wanted to make sure this theme is restated here. It was important to
Jesus, so it was important to Luke.

Jesus began to teach the people in parables. These stories were easy for
them to remember and had at least two layers of understanding. For those
who sought to understand the word of God, they would discover the true
meaning behind the story. Those, however, who merely listened or who
were enemies of His mission would not comprehend it, hearing the story
but only understanding it on its surface. These parables would also act to

deflect direct accusations from members of the latter group because they would lack any concrete statements to use against Him.

The parable of the sower is recorded in all three of the synoptic gospels. At that time, seed was first thrown and then tilled into the soil. Inevitably, some landed in places other than the field, making for an ideal analogy for Jesus' story. He finished the story with a challenge to those listening, to grasp and understand His meaning and not let the words go in one ear and out the other. When His disciples asked the meaning of the parable, Jesus quoted Isaiah 6:9 to explain why He taught in parables. Those who do not want to see will not; those who do not want to understand will not. As He later makes clear,

> Luke 11:9-10
> **"So I say to you: ask and it will be given to you; seek and you will find; knock and the door will be opened to you. For everyone who asks receives; the one who seeks finds; and to the one who knocks, the door will be opened."**

This parable was not the only time Jesus had used a seed to represent the word of God. Later, He used the mustard seed to make a different point, and at another time, He pointed out that unless the seed "died" and was buried, there would be no new plant/growth. Knowing His fate and subsequent glorification through the resurrection, He being the true Word of God, was purposeful in his use of the seed in these illustrations.

The lessons of this parable are many. Jesus did not shy from talking about the devil working actively in the world against the word of God and preventing people from understanding it and drawing closer to God. There are always those who react emotionally, receiving the word, saying they believe it, but when tested, they fail because they do not have the will to stand up to temptation. Belief is a matter of will, not feeling. To become a disciple of Jesus Christ, a person must make a commitment to Him, not simply bask in the sunshine of the gospel.

Unfortunately, the seed among thorns represents much of what we see today (and have always seen), when people make their commitment in the heat of the moment, only to compromise step-by-step with the pressures and distractions of society, thereby diluting their focus on Christ until He receives the attention they have left over after everything else. Those who persevere do not compromise but remain steadfast in their commitment and continue to mature as disciples, producing a crop of other believers as a result of their faithfulness.

Jesus then told his disciples that a lamp had been lit. The light, the truth, should not be hidden from sight but put up high for all to see. Indeed, there is nothing hidden that will not be disclosed. The light will eventually shine everywhere and expose everyone and everything. He instructed them that they should listen carefully so they could speak the truth. Whoever does understand the truth will be given more understanding. He who comes up with his own ideas will lose what little he has. Listen well, learn the truth well, and put the light up high where all can see–tell the truth to everyone.

We know from other gospels that Jesus' family came to see Him out of concern that He was "out of his mind" (Mark 3:31-32) and that His brothers didn't believe in Him at the time (John 7:5). Luke preferred to focus on the primary message, however, which is that the spiritual supersedes the physical. Obedience to God's word takes precedence over all other relationships. Jesus did not mean He didn't love his family, but He wanted to clearly make this point clear to the crowd and his disciples. Likewise, he did not want his family to divert him from His mission. Jesus was doing the same when He said that John the Baptist was the "greatest born of women," yet the least in the Kingdom of God was greater than he. Jesus continued to emphasize this more important perspective.

One day, Jesus wanted to go to the other side of the lake. Given where they were, in Galilee, crossing the north end of the lake would be a short trip, and taking the boats would be the logical way to get there. After all, most of his disciples were fishermen. It would be a trip of just a few miles. The lake, however, was notorious for having sudden storms with steep embankments on both sides and a cold, deep undercurrent. The gale they found themselves in was actually flooding the boats, which were fairly shallow. These were experienced men on the boats, and they recognized the seriousness of the situation and were genuinely afraid. Jesus, on the other hand, was fast asleep. Once awakened, He ordered the wind and waves to subside, and they did—the sea became calm.

Ah, but then Jesus asked His disciples, "Where is your faith?" They were all wondering who was this man who could command the waves and wind, and they obeyed! Faith in what? Faith in whom? Exactly the point. Jesus was trying to get them to see Him for who He was. He had been giving them glimpses of His glory, though they failed to understand. Power over nature was a clear sign of the power of God. The miracles leading the Hebrews out of Egypt were a testimony of that same power. If they truly understood who Jesus was, then they would not have feared anything, knowing they were in the hands of the ever-loving, all-powerful God.

They completed their journey and arrived at the region of Garasenes. This place represented the other side of the tracks, Gentile territory. This event was so full of symbolism that many believe it was metaphorical, yet it is told in all three synoptic gospels, though with slight variations. Plus, Matthew and Mark were there. It is entirely possible that Jesus intentionally took His disciples away from their familiar world to "the other side" for this event in order to isolate it and manifest within it all the layers of meaning so they would retain the knowledge forever. Obviously, that plan worked, with two of the eye-witnesses recording the story in their gospels and Luke understanding its importance and reporting it as well.

Jesus was immediately met by a man. This man was the lowest form of humanity, most depraved. He was naked, which was socially unacceptable, particularly when meeting someone and especially when meeting a rabbi. He was loud and rude. He lived among the tombs, which made him unclean. The demons had forced him to live there to torment him with the natural fear of the dead and the spiritually dead. He was deprived of the basic necessities of life: clothing and shelter and probably allowed only enough food to keep him alive. His was not a temporary situation but a long-termed one. Chronic, per Luke, a medical term. He was well known, and the demons were well entrenched.

Jesus ordered the demon to come out, and they responded, for they knew who Jesus was. They used the term "Most High God," a term used by the Gentiles. Evil was encountering the divine. This encounter was spiritual warfare at a high level. There was great fear. Jesus wanted to know his name, for to know the name was the first step toward mastering the man or the demon. To show who was in control, the demons answered, "Legion," which can mean as many as 6,000, or it could mean they represented legions of demons allied against Jesus. Either way, a formidable force was engaged in this war.

Yet the demons knew their ultimate fate and begged Jesus not to order them into the Abyss, the place of confinement for their kind and Satan. They also knew Jesus' authority. "Pigs are unclean for Jews, so put us there," meaning they would wait until He was gone and then seek another to torment. Demons need a body to live in to afflict evil. When Jesus allowed them to go into the pigs, the swine then ran down the hill into the lake and drown. Who was in control? The pigs' demise was reminiscent of the drowning of Pharaoh's army. Another interpretation is that Satan led the pigs to slaughter in order to inflict economic damage on the people since he couldn't on the man, hoping doing so would thwart Jesus' attempt at ministry in the region.

Indeed, the swineherds reported the event and put the blame on Jesus (certainly not on themselves). The people of the region went to see for themselves and found their world upside down. The pigs were, in fact, gone and the man who had always been a raving maniac was sitting, clothed, and talking sensibly. They were faced with a miracle, an encounter with the divine, and were overcome with fear. They asked Jesus to leave, which He quietly did. They were more concerned with the status quo than the salvation of the man. He, on the other hand, wanted to go with Jesus, to cling to this new life, but Jesus told him to go home and tell the good news. The miracle-worker Jesus would not get confused with the misreading of the scriptures of what the Messiah would be like in this Gentile territory. No reason to keep this miracle a secret. The homeless man, estranged from society, had been restored and could now return home. He had a story to tell. We all have a story to tell.

Jesus and his followers went back to Capernaum, where they were met by a crowd waiting for Him. Jairus, one of the leaders at the synagogue, interrupted the scene by falling at Jesus' feet, begging him to come to his house because his twelve-year-old daughter was dying. Of course,

Jesus agreed to go and made His way through the crowd, but as He was going toward this spontaneous journey of mercy, yet another interruption occurred.

A woman who had been bleeding ("hemorrhaging" is the term Luke the physician uses) for twelve years was in the crowd. She had spent everything she had seeking a cure, but none of the doctors could find a cure. Her condition made her ritually impure, preventing her from entering the synagogue and isolating her from her religious and cultural community. After all this time and with her savings spent, she was totally laid waste, spiritually, emotionally, and physically. In desperation, she reached out to touch Jesus' cloak, and when she did, the bleeding stopped. It is when we are at our weakest that God most evidently exhibits His grace. As the Lord told Paul, when he pleaded for relief of the thorn in his flesh:

2 Corinthians 12:9
"My grace is sufficient for you, for my power is made perfect in weakness."

Jesus knew immediately the power of the Holy Spirit had passed through him. He probably knew to whom, why, and the result, but again He wanted to make this a teaching moment for everyone there, including the woman. Yes, the crowd was all around, pushing and shoving, but this touch was an intentional one seeking mercy. He let her tell her story, which she did with all humility, called her "daughter," and pronounced her healed because of her faith. Shalom. A great lesson in faith indeed, but the greater lesson was yet to come.

While this diversion occupied Jesus' time, word came that Jairus' daughter had died. Jesus called on Jairus' faith, "Just believe, and she will be healed." Jesus limited the witnesses to the parents and His closest disciples. He quieted the mourners. Unlike the stormy seas, they laughed at Him, thinking they knew better than He. No matter. Truth would soon speak for itself. He gently called the girl by her name after taking her hand, and her "breath returned." She must eat. She probably hadn't eaten in several days, plus ghosts did not eat, and eating would prove she was indeed alive. The parents were understandably ecstatic, but Jesus told them to keep her revival secret.

Both of the daughters here were marginalized members of society. One because she was ritually unclean; the other because she was just coming of age to be an adult but dying. The girl was twelve-years-old; the other had been suffering the length of the girl's life. Both were saved. It would appear at one point in the story that one was saved at the expense of the other, but Jesus tells Jairus to not be afraid, to trust. The extra time spent healing the bleeding woman did not endanger his daughter.

Time spent with God does not detract from other things. God always allows time for Him. Somehow, there is always enough time for all the other things if we take the time to be in the presence of God. It always works. This is the greater lesson.

This is also one of God's Great Promises. **God faithfully promises His presence**. If we seek Him out, He is there, anywhere, whenever.

Isaiah 55:6
Seek the Lord while he may be found;
call on him while he is near.

Jeremiah 29:13
"You will seek me and find me when you seek me with all your heart."

CHAPTER NINE

J esus then determined it was time for a new phase of the ministry, a time for the apostles to step up and perform the acts Jesus had been doing: driving out demons, curing diseases, preaching the Kingdom of God. Jesus gave them the authority to do these things. They were for the first time, acting in their full capacity as His ambassadors, representing the Son of God and enabled to perform miracles in His name. They were to proclaim God's kingdom.

They were to take nothing with them, not even the usual provisions, but be dependent upon those to whom they would be ministering. Be dependent on God. This dependence would also make them distinctly different from less reputable wandering preachers. The point of staying in the first house was to show no favoritism, not to look like they were seeking a better place to stay but to be content with what was offered. Shaking the dust from one's sandals was a traditional sign of rejection, separation from anything to do with the place. The apostles apparently left immediately, obediently, and fulfilled their duty, covering a lot of territory.

Herod, always keeping his ear to the ground, paranoid that he was, heard what was going on. He was confused. He had beheaded John, but he was hearing all kinds of rumors: John is back from the dead, Elijah had returned, or one of the other prophets had returned. He tried to see who this man was who was causing such a stir in his kingdom, not knowing it was a cadre of empowered apostles all acting through the power of the Holy Spirit.

The apostles returned from their mission, telling Jesus what they had done. Jesus wanted some quality time with them, so they tried to sneak away to a small town on the outskirts, to Bethsaida on the northeast corner of the lake. The crowd, however, figured out where they were and followed them. Jesus compassionately welcomed them, taught them about God's kingdom, and healed those who need healing. That's who He was.

Late in the day, the Twelve advised Jesus to send the crowds away so they could go find provisions for themselves for supper. They were being practical. It was a remote place, and the people needed to get to the neighboring villages before dark to buy food. It was the logical thing to do. Jesus' response was simple: "You give them something to eat," but they had so little, just five loaves of bread and two fish. They had just been on a journey, depending on others to feed them. What they had wasn't even enough for themselves. The crowd was huge, about 5,000 men. If their wives and children were counted, too, the total must have been more like 12-15,000.

Jesus took the lead. He knew what He was going to do. He told them to have the people sit in groups of roughly fifty each, reminiscent of the regimented groups of the Israelites in the wilderness. Jesus is God, and He was about to feed His people manna. The disciples obeyed, and the people obeyed. Luke tells this story with absolute brevity.

Jesus acted as the host, taking the food, breaking it, and giving thanks: "Blessed are you, oh Lord, our God, King of the world, who brings forth bread from the earth"—the traditional Jewish blessing. The food was then distributed. All ate, and all were satisfied. Leftovers were gathered, which filled twelve baskets, one for each of the tribes of Israel.

This unmitigated miracle is one of only two (the other being the resurrection) recorded in all four gospels. The broken bread, benefiting all, also foreshadows the Last Supper, where the New Covenant was established: Jesus' body broken for the sake of all.

Luke now shifts to a completely different scene, a most important one, in which Jesus and his disciples were alone together. Jesus was praying but then turned and asked who the crowds said He was. Luke's focus on who Jesus was has been leading up to this moment. The disciples had seen

Him as a companion, teacher, healer, miracle worker. He even commanded the wind and waves! He cast out demons, forgave sins, and raised a girl from the dead. The crowds had seen just a glimpse of these miracles. The crowds saw the teacher and the healer. Some of them thought John the Baptist had been resurrected, others said Elijah, and still others thought Him another prophet from long ago. But Jesus wanted to know what the disciples thought.

Peter was not only the spokesman, but also it was his very nature to be reactive, to jump out there, and to speak first. He spoke from the heart and proclaimed Jesus to be the Messiah, the Anointed One, and the Deliverer. Luke did not record Jesus' commendation of Peter's statement, nor did he write about Peter's attempt to prevent Jesus from going toward Jerusalem. Instead, he focused on Jesus' clarification to the disciples of what Messiah means because there was a lot of misunderstanding. Most Jews would have told you the Messiah would come as a commander of heavenly armies to drive out the oppressors (Romans) and re-establish Israel in her rightful place as God's favored country. Jesus, however, painted a very different picture for them, introducing the suffering Messiah, even outlining for them details of what will happen. Therefore, it was important that this truth be kept a secret at the time, so the crowds would not get the wrong idea about who Jesus was and what His mission was.

While Jesus had their undivided attention, He taught them the very kernel of what it meant to be one of his disciples. This lesson is in all four gospels, and it can also be found in the gospel of Thomas and Q. No other message of Jesus is written in such strong language. It is pointedly personal, singular, and meant to be taken without exception. Taken together, these verses (23–26) are the very core of His teaching. Luke very intentionally defines discipleship right after establishing Jesus' identity as Christ.

Jesus started with the self. It must die. Each one must take up his own cross, dismissing the life that will be lost because of it—an act of will, not an emotion. He emphasized daily because this is a decision one must make each day, though this point is made only in Luke. By giving up one's self, one can be generous with what material things one has. Giving up selfish wants results in providing for the needs of the greater good. Putting one's self last makes one humble and gives one a servant's attitude.

By giving up the life they were used to living in this world, the disciples would then save their eternal lives, living as children of God. Worldly success, as they had known it—the reward of being good and obeying the Law, would gain nothing if the soul were lost. The shame Jesus speaks of is the hesitation of not being totally openly committed to Him through willing obedience.

Nothing in this teaching violates God's Word. It can't and it doesn't. God had been speaking through his prophets for centuries these truths, culminating in the two commands that summarize all the prophets and the Law:

Matthew 22:37
"You must love the Lord your God with all your heart, with all your being, and with all your mind."

Matthew 22:39
"You must love your neighbor as you love yourself."

The closing comment of Jesus' discourse has been interpreted in many ways, though most scholars believe it is a reference to the transfiguration, which follows chronologically in Luke. Others think it alludes to the coming of the Holy Spirit at Pentecost, while there are those who think it simply means the development of the Church in their time, the Kingdom of God growing among humanity.

Luke gives us no indication of the disciples' reaction to this teaching. He transports us instead to roughly a week later. "Eight days" was a conventional way of saying it was more than a week and a Sabbath but less than two weeks. Jesus again took just Peter, John, and James with Him for a spiritual encounter. It's always fascinating to read how first century writers attempt to describe the indescribable. Jesus' appearance changed, even His clothes. While praying, humbling Himself, He was exalted.

Somehow, the men knew it was Moses and Elijah that were with Him, both "clothed in heavenly splendor," talking about Jesus' "departure" in Jerusalem. Moses was there, representing the Law. Moses, the Deliverer, a job completed by another Joshua. Elijah represented the prophets. His mission was also completed by another: Elisha, an alternate name for Joshua. Here they stand with God's Messiah, Jesus, whose Jewish name is Joshua. As Moses delivered God's people from bondage, so Jesus would lead all people to freedom: Jesus, the fulfillment of prophecy. No other needed to follow Him to finish His work. He would finish it on the cross, where He would Himself declare, "It is finished!"

Peter and the other two were apparently quite sleepy. It was not unusual for Jesus to pray late into the night or all night, so most likely it was late. Somehow, they managed to stay awake and witness this divine event. Peter, being Peter, blurted out something irrational about building some temporary shrines for them. Sleep deprivation or thin air (remember Peter was a fisherman from Galilee) can make a person act a little stupid. God intervened with a cloud and wiped away the notion; Moses and Elijah disappeared and left only Jesus and His three apostles. The cloud "overshadowed" them in the same way the Holy Spirit overcame Mary at Jesus' conception. They were in awe, being held for the moment in a touch of God's glory.

Then God spoke! What He said was much like what is recorded at Jesus' baptism, but these three heard Him say it directly to them, so there is no doubt. This is God's son. Every word He says is precious and should be coveted. It is no wonder they were speechless. They were left with Jesus alone. No one else was needed. They would keep this experience to themselves for now.

Luke spends some time, in the next few sections, illustrating how little the disciples truly understood who Jesus was, what His mission was, and even the essence of what He had been teaching. While we may have wondered how, after living day-to-day with Jesus for what we think is almost three years, these men could not better understand. They were uneducated people who had learned from their rabbis what they knew about scripture. They had preconceived notions about a Messiah that had been distorted by the Pharisees and Scribes and passed on to the rabbis.

Much of what they witnessed they simply did not understand and could not put into perspective. They kept waiting for Jesus to explain everything, but Jesus taught in parables. Even when he explained the parables to them, they still could not connect the dots.

Large crowds now followed Jesus everywhere, seeking miracles and healing. When they came down from the mountain, many were there waiting for him. One man was desperate, for his only son was possessed, and the disciples could not exorcise the demon. Jesus, just having touched the realm of the divine, was suddenly thrust back into the depraved world of Satan. The people did not yet have a Savior in which to believe, so they remained ignorant and perverse (as we shall see in the next section, so were the disciples). The demon gave his best effort for the crowd, but Jesus rebuked it, and the demon left. Luke always notes the human side, that Jesus gives the son back to the father, the child being his only son. Jesus well understood. The people, on the other hand, were overwhelmed by **God's** greatness.

Jesus again took the opportunity to put things into proper context. The disciples were beaming with this great success, and He needed to bring them down to earth so they could understand the reality of the suffering Messiah. For the second time, Jesus explained clearly what would happen. Luke says the meaning was hidden from them, and they were afraid to ask for clarity. What Jesus said made no sense to them, but they had developed such respect for Him that they dared not ask Him to explain. They were ashamed they couldn't understand, but they were afraid to ask.

Luke goes on to illustrate further how the disciples had not grasped Jesus' message. Luke puts this story in juxtaposition to Jesus just having told the disciples about his coming suffering. (Other gospels put the story in a different place and time.) Here, they were talking about being exalted to great positions of power. Luke carefully points out that Jesus was "aware of their deepest thoughts."

Jesus took a little child, one with no rights and valued very little in society, the least important, and had him stand next to Him. Welcoming someone was the indication of hospitality, highly valued in the culture of the day. Jesus would use hospitality in future parables. People would go to great lengths to make sure a guest was well taken care of and provided for. Here again, Jesus turns things around. Welcome a child! That would be the same as welcoming Jesus? And that would be the same as welcoming the Father? All the lessons in the Hebrew Scriptures about humility had been lost, and Jesus was saying they were paramount.

What Jesus did in this case was instead of telling a parable, He acted out a parable. To welcome a child would be to do so without any expectation of anything in return, no reward. Prominence is not important. Relationship is what is important, and humility is the appropriate approach.

Even John, one of the inner circle, got this message wrong. He stepped in, wanting to prove that he understood, by telling Jesus they told a man to stop using Jesus' name to drive out demons, "because he is not one of us." Jesus knew how many enemies His disciples, then and later, would face. Persecution is an ugly thing. He cautioned them not to worry about the man. "Who is not against you is for you."

Verse 51 is a turning point in Luke. The author writes about only one trip to Jerusalem, though we know there were three trips over the three years of Jesus' ministry. Luke's gospel is more thematic and wraps up these trips into one, even though it is somewhat circuitous. The King James Version (KJV) and even the New King James Version (NKJV) state, "He steadfastly set His face to go to Jerusalem." It was a very definite, determined decision, a pivotal moment in history when Jesus moved from his healing and teaching ministry toward His inevitable suffering, death, and resurrection. This is why Luke prefaces the paragraph the way he does, referring to Jesus being taken up to heaven. Everything changed from this point on. There was no stopping Him. This was the Father's plan, and Jesus was totally obedient to His Father.

Jesus sent messengers ahead, a common practice, which we will see again at the Triumphal Entry into Jerusalem. They were to "get things ready for Him," which is to say they were politely to request accommodations. The messengers Jesus sent ahead got to a Samaritan village where they were summarily rejected because His troupe was headed to Jerusalem. Why?

The hatred between the Jews and the Samaritans went back to the days of Ezra and Nehemiah, when the Jews returned from Babylonian captivity to rebuild Jerusalem and the temple. The Samaritans were Jews who had been left behind. They had intermarried with the locals. These unions made them impure in the eyes of the Jews, who were trying to re-establish a true, pure Jewish state. The Samaritans were driven out of Jerusalem. Any Jew who had married outside his religion had to send his wife and children away. The Samaritans settled north of Jerusalem in the hills of Judea. The hatred grew over time, such that a good Jew would not even set foot in Samaria. He would rather travel on the east side of the Jordan River and circumvent Samaria in order to avoid it. Pilgrims headed toward Jerusalem would normally also avoid Samaria, and Jesus and his followers appeared to be just another group of Jewish pilgrims to these Samaritans.

The Samaritan's hatred of the Jews was culminated in their hatred of Jerusalem. The Jews preached that it was only in Jerusalem that could be found the house of God, where He could be worshiped, where sacrifices were honored, and where prayers were heard. The Samaritans believed Samaria was just as good or better. If these men were Jews on their way to Jerusalem, then they wanted no part of them.

The brothers, James and John, having once on their appointed mission trip experienced the power of the Holy Spirit and being incensed by the rejection of the Samaritans, wanted to call down fire from heaven and destroy them. They felt perfectly within their rights to ask Jesus for permission. Instead of receiving approval, they were rebuked. Such actions were not consistent with what Jesus had been teaching for almost three years.

Just as the disciples didn't understand much of the time, so many others did not understand what it meant to be a disciple of Jesus, either then or now. Luke illustrates this reality in his next section, showing how everyday life interferes with commitment.

The first encounter was with a man who declared his intent with an absolutist statement that he would follow Jesus wherever He went. Jesus made it clear that even the wild animals had places they called home, but He did not (at least not yet). This illustration could also be interpreted as meaning Jesus had no possessions, that He had rejected material things, lived in abject poverty, dependent upon the generosity of others.

To another, Jesus extended an invitation to join them, but He is told he must wait to bury his father. Given that the Jews bury their dead the next day after they die, his was a thinly veiled excuse to wait until a more convenient time. "Let me wait until Dad dies, I get his inheritance, get the kids out of the house, get the wife settled, and the business sold; then, I can come and join you."

Jesus responded, "Let those that are spiritually dead bury the dead. Those that are spiritually alive should be busy now proclaiming the good news."

The third man in Luke's illustration just wanted to go say good-bye to his family first. Jesus' replied, "Do not come until you are ready to make a full, unconditional commitment. Do not start something you will not stay with and finish with all your heart."

CHAPTER TEN

J esus again sent out His followers as messengers—"to every town and place where he was about to go." This time He expanded the group beyond the Twelve. The ancient transcripts vary whether the number was seventy or seventy-two. A case could be made for either. Seventy-two could represent three pairs for each of the twelve tribes of Israel. More likely, however, seventy is the same as the number of Elders of Israel (ref. Exodus / Numbers 11:16, 17, 24, 25), as well as the number of members in the Sanhedrin. It was also commonly believed there were seventy nations in the world at the time—a whole and complete number, adequate for the task at hand. They were to go to every town and city between where He was and Jerusalem.

Jesus sent them out two by two. He also sent out the apostles in pairs (Luke 9:1-6). This was so they could encourage each other. Their abilities would complement the other, and one could help the other if he needed help.

Ecclesiastes 4:9&10:
Two are better than one because they have a good return for their work: If one falls down, his friend can help him up.

The early church followed this pattern.
Acts:
13:2   Barnabas and Paul
15:27   Judas and Silas
39-40   Barnabas and Mark; Paul and Silas

17:14   Silas and Timothy
19:22   Timothy and Erastus

As before, the disciples were to depend on those to whom they were sent, letting God provide their needs. There would be many souls where they would be going, and their experiences would be just the start of evangelism, for the Word had not yet spread. The prayer was for more workers to go out and witness, for it was God's will that all be saved.

> 1 Timothy 2:3-4
> This is good and pleases God our Savior, who wants all men to be saved and to come to a knowledge of the truth.

The disciples would be as lambs because there would be wolves where they were being sent. They are lambs, gentle, like those sacrificed for others.

It is interesting that Jesus told them to not take sandals with them. They had to rely on the ones they were wearing to last, just as the ones the Israelites wore through the wilderness for forty years never wore out.

And it would be violating common courtesy to not greet others on the road. The mission, therefore, was deemed such a high priority that such niceties must be set aside to keep the sense of urgency and pace required. There was precedent for this type of behavior:

> 2 Kings 4:29
> Elisha said to Gehazi, "Tuck your cloak into your belt, take my staff in your hand and run. If you meet anyone, do not greet him, and if anyone greets you, do not answer."

To offer "Shalom" to a house upon entering was to grant peace to all within. They were not to move around, for it would appear they were seeking better accommodations. Likewise, they were to eat what was provided and not be demanding. The directions Jesus gave them were simple: heal the sick and preach of the coming of the Kingdom of God. If the town rejected them, it would suffer later for their decision. Again, this teaching is consistent with Luke's understanding of the gospel. Truth is presented; it is up to one to accept or reject it and deal with the consequences.

Jesus then proceeded to illustrate a basic principle: rejection of the truth is worse than continuing in ignorant sin. Korazin and Bethsaida had heard the good news, yet had not embraced it. Capernaum, where Jesus had spent so much time and produced many miracles, continued to live as it had. Tyre and Sidon, on the other hand, were in territories outside Jesus' ministry.

Jesus told His disciples that those who listened to them listened to Him. He would be speaking through them. The Holy Spirit was already at work. Those who rejected them rejected Jesus and He who sent Him.

Joy, on the other hand, is the inevitable result of salvation. Over and over, we see joy associated with salvation in Luke's writings, in both his gospel and in The Acts of the Apostles. The disciples returned from their appointed mission not with fatigue but with overwhelming joy. There is no joy greater than fulfilling a divine mission. The demons submitted to Jesus' name; the glory is His. Satan was indeed hurt by the disciples' mission. The disciples of the Son of God are effectively leading people back to God. Jesus sees Satan fall from his self-appointed throne over earth; the fall is dramatic, sudden, like lightning. This fall is the beginning of the end for Satan. People, enabled by the power of the Holy Spirit, were advancing the Kingdom of God on earth.

Jesus explained to the disciples that they really had more power and authority than they knew. They had everything they needed to overcome Satan.

Matthew 13:12
"Whoever has will be given more, and he will have an abundance."

Their obedience to His two simple commandments would lead to more. But a word of caution. True glory comes only from what God has done for you, not what you have done for God.

Casting out demons is not nearly as important as being saved yourself, with your name written in the (Lamb's) Book of Life: Psalm 69:28; Daniel 12:1; Philippians 4:3; Hebrews 12:23; Revelation 3:5; John 1:12.

To all who received Him, to those who believed in His name, He gave the right to become children of God.

Jesus was also full of joy, as the Son of God, the effector of the Holy Spirit. He praised the Father for His plan of working through ordinary people rather than the Pharisees, Scribes, and "experts in the law." He then turned to His followers, explained, and tried to put God's plan into perspective for them. We cannot read these words without thinking that we too would like to have seen Him and heard Him in this moment.

Luke sets up the Parable of the Good Samaritan as a separate entity. The legal expert suddenly appeared and asked Jesus an often-debated question, one of those discussed by his peers. The question was framed in a somewhat challenging manner, though, in that he added "eternal" to life. It also was based on the understanding of salvation by works. The Hebrew Scriptures did talk about achieving, earning, or inheriting life. Luke makes it clear that the legal expert presented the question as a test. Here he was, the learned scholar, against this back-roads (uneducated) preacher.

Probably much to the legal expert's surprise, Jesus responded much as a seasoned rabbi would: by asking him a related question. This counter question would be an accepted practice and entirely appropriate for a rabbi in good standing. Jesus essentially said, "Okay, you're the expert in the law, so you tell me. What does the law say, and how do you interpret it?" Recovering his balance, the lawyer, eager to show off his grasp of scripture, readily stated the two most fundamental codes of Jewish law that he knew relate to life. If they relate to life, surely they must relate to eternal life (crossing his fingers). Jesus maintained the upper role of teacher by affirming the answer. His answer, if the man was sharp enough to discern it, was in fact scripture.

Leviticus 18:5

"Keep my decrees and laws, for the man who obeys them will live by them. I am the LORD"

The lawyer, however, was not satisfied. He did not get Jesus to say anything for which He could be criticized. He didn't get Jesus on the defensive. In fact, he was on the defensive himself, so he needed to push a little more, a little harder. "Who is my neighbor?" Now the commonly held belief among Jews was that only other Jews were their neighbors. All Gentiles were "fuel for the fires of hell." In spite of the teachings of Hebrew Scripture:

Leviticus 24:22
"You are to have the same law for the alien and the native-born. I am the LORD your God."

Numbers 15:15-16
"The community is to have the same rules for you and for the alien living among you; this is a lasting ordinance for the generations to come. You and the alien shall be the same before the LORD: the same laws and regulations will apply both to you and to the alien living among you. "

Leviticus 19:34
"The alien living with you must be treated as one of your native-born. Love him as yourself..."

Against this backdrop, Jesus told a story, a parable, probably one of the most well-known of all.

The man going to Jericho from Jerusalem would be assumed to be a Jew. That's who traveled that path for the most part, so the listeners would automatically think he was a Jew. This man was mugged. The path was somewhat treacherous, and there were many areas where travelers could be surprised by bandits. They take everything but his life.

The first person to find the victim is a priest. He carefully passes by on the other side of the road. Was he afraid the man was dead, and he would become unclean if he touched him? Was he on his way to Jerusalem to serve in the temple, a chance he wouldn't get again for years, if ever? If he is unclean, he wouldn't be able to serve. A priest was one of the most respected members of Jewish society. He must have had some good, selfish reason for simply passing by. Perhaps he was afraid it was a trap, and he himself might get mugged.

The second person to find the man was a Levite, a lay leader of the church, also well respected for his special role as designated by the Law by God Himself. Yet he too past by and abandoned the man, and we are left to wonder why.

The third person to find him was a Samaritan. You could just hear the people in the crowd listening to Jesus gasp when He made that statement. What was a Samaritan even doing on that road? Samaritans were just half-breeds, both physically and spiritually; however, it was this Samaritan who had compassion for the man. He came to him, as opposed to passing by him. He did all he could do for him, took him to the inn, and further cared for him there. He used his own oil and wine, good medicine to fight infection and pain. He put him on his donkey while he walked. He took time from his travels to tend to him. There was obviously a level of trust between the Samaritan and the innkeeper, such that he left him in his trust, along with about $400, which should have been more than enough, but with a promise to compensate for any additional expenses. What more could he have done? All these things he did, giving of himself to help another. Self-sacrifice for another's needs. He saw beyond any racial differences to see a person in need, had pity on him, and did everything he could to help him.

Jesus then asked, "Which of these three do you think was a neighbor to the man who fell in the hands of robbers?" The legal expert who started this dialogue could not bring himself to say "Samaritan," so he replied, "The one who had mercy on him."

Luke's positioning of this parable here is intentional. It follows just after Jesus' remarks after the seventy return:

Luke 10:21b
"I praise you, Father, Lord of heaven and earth, because you have hidden these things from the wise and learned, and revealed them to little children. Yes, Father, for this is what you were pleased to do."

The priest, the Levite, and this legal scholar would be the "wise and intelligent," certainly not the Samaritan. The Samaritan was not encumbered by their learning and legalism, just a good, simple, and honest man who did the right thing. He lacked the prejudice of the priest and Levite, not unlike the prejudice of the legal expert questioning Jesus. They both consider themselves righteous when in fact it was the Samaritan who was righteous as shown by his actions.

Matthew 25:34-40
"Then the King will say to those on his right, 'Come, you who are blessed by my Father; take your inheritance, the kingdom prepared for you since the creation of the world. For I was hungry and you gave me something to eat, I was thirsty and you gave me something to drink, I was a stranger and you invited me in, I needed clothes and you clothed me, I was sick and you looked after me, I was in prison and you came to visit me.'

"Then the righteous will answer him, 'Lord, when did we see you hungry and feed you, or thirsty and give you something to drink? When did we see you a stranger and invite you in, or needing clothes and clothe you? When did we see you sick or in prison and go to visit you?'

"The King will reply, 'I tell you the truth, whatever you did for one of the least of these brothers of mine, you did for me.'

Luke rather abruptly cuts back to the trip to Jerusalem, where Jesus and his followers were at Bethany, about two miles from Jerusalem. Martha asked Jesus to stay with her, and He accepted. Her sister Mary was with her. Mary was enthralled with what Jesus was saying and sat at His feet, totally taken in by His words. Martha, on the other hand, was completely occupied with the business of hospitality. After all, this was her house, and she had invited Jesus and His folks there. Besides, providing appropriate hospitality was very important. She quickly became overwhelmed with the chores and took offense at her sister's apparent laziness, just sitting there while she did all the work. Instead of gesturing to Mary or trying to get her attention or even whispering to her, she goes straight to Jesus and complains.

Jesus' response was to invoke Martha's name twice, which was a common manner of speaking when one person wanted to make sure one had the other's attention. It can also be used in a manner of endearment. Here, it could easily had been taken either way. Yes, Martha was consumed by the details of preparation for the guests, but Jesus tells her there was really only one thing that was necessary. Mary had chosen what was better, and it would not be denied her. "You, Martha, may be all tied up with good intentions, paying attention to all the details, but here in your room sits the Son of God, speaking God's word, and Mary has elected to sit and take it all in." As He told Satan in the wilderness, when He quoted from Deuteronomy 8:3,

> Man does not live on bread alone but on every word that comes from the mouth of the LORD.

CHAPTER ELEVEN

L uke now takes us through some of Jesus' teachings before the final entry into Jerusalem.

The first is about prayer. This is something His disciples had seen Him doing consistently for all the time they had been with Him and could see how important it was to Him. Prayer was an absolute necessity for Jesus. Through it, He communed with the Father and received the power of the Holy Spirit.

> John 14:10
> **"Don't you believe that I am in the Father, and that the Father is in me? The words I say to you are not just my own authority. Rather, it is the Father, living in me, who is doing his work."**

Because,

> John 5:19
> **"I tell you the truth, the Son can do nothing by himself..."**

Luke's phrase, "One of the disciples," was a nice way not to single out any one of the disciples but let the request, a prayer in itself, be generic. The disciple's request asked, "Lord, teach us to pray, just as John taught his disciples." Perhaps, the disciple had been a disciple of John the Baptist before he was imprisoned, for it was not unusual for disciples of any rabbi to ask for guidance for prayer. Jesus complied by offering no parable, no hidden meanings, just a clear model, easily remembered.

"Father." Jesus started the prayer the same way He would start His own prayer. "Abba" was the familiar term for father, putting us in the position of His children, emphasizing our relationship with God as reborn and with each other as brothers and sisters.

> Romans 8:16&17
> The Spirit himself testifies with our spirit that we are God's children. Now if we are children, then we are heirs—heirs of God and co-heirs with Christ...

> Galatians 4:6
> Because you are sons, God sent the Spirit of his Son into our hearts, the Spirit who calls out, "Abba, Father."

It was one thing for Jesus to call God Father, quite another for us to. To begin prayer invoking Abba's name was a new concept for the disciples, probably a shock to think of God as approachable. To them, God was always so holy that people could not even speak His name! Yet Jesus had said they had to become as children...

The CEB translation says, "Uphold the holiness of your name." The power of one's name cannot be over-emphasized, especially when considering the name of God. One of the commandments given to Moses by God was not to take the name of the LORD in vain. It was that important to God and was to be that important to the people. There was power in a name. To know one's name was to have power over that person. This fact is one of the reasons Jesus often asked the name of a demon He was about to exorcise. It is obvious then why we cannot know the true name of God. We are left with "I AM." The very power of God protects His name. In this prayer, Jesus says we should acknowledge the absolute primacy of God by His name and its holiness.

"Your kingdom come," or "Bring in your kingdom." Many translations follow this petition with, "May your will be done on earth as it is in heaven." These two requests, taken together, would be a typical couplet with the second sentence meaning the same as the first, just reinforcing the idea. Couplets are used extensively in Psalms and Proverbs. By praying this way, the disciple is asking God to effect His kingdom on earth—a new and wonderful world replacing the old.

Revelation 21:1
Then I saw a new heaven and a new earth, for the first heaven and the first earth had passed away.

Isaiah 65: 17&18a
"Behold, I will create
new heavens and a new earth.
The former things will not be remembered,
nor will they come to mind.
But be glad and rejoice forever
in what I will create..."

In this prayer, believers are putting themselves in alignment with God's will, God's plan, which is manifested in the world by the actions of the believer—the way one treats others. Do you love your neighbor as you love yourself? Do you do to others as you would like them to do to you?

"Give us each day our daily bread." Stop now and notice that Jesus has first included the Kingdom of God and daily bread: two of the temptations he faced while being tempted in the wilderness by Satan. These are very basic elements to the human experience.

Now again, "Give us each day our daily bread." A clear reminder of the imagery of God providing manna to the Israelites in the wilderness. The manna, given fresh each day, was sufficient for that day. Our prayer then is to trust God to provide what is needed for each day.

Matthew 6:19-34
"Do not store up for yourselves treasures on earth, where
moth and rust destroy, and where thieves break in and
steal. But store up for yourselves treasures in heaven, where
moth and rust do not destroy, and where thieves do not
break in and steal. For where your treasure is, there your
heart will be also.

"The eye is the lamp of the body. If your eyes are good, your whole body will be full of light. But if your eyes are bad, your whole body will be full of darkness. If then the light within you is darkness, how great is that darkness!

"No one can serve two masters. Either he will hate the one and love the other, or he will be devoted to the one and despise the other. You cannot serve both God and Money.

"Therefore, I tell you, do not worry about your life, what you will eat or drink; or about your body, what you will wear. Is not life more important than food, and the body more important than clothes? Look at the birds of the air; they do not sow or reap or store away in barns, and yet your heavenly Father feeds them. Are you not much more valuable than they? Who of you by worrying can add a single hour to his life?

"And why do you worry about clothes? See how the lilies of the field grow. They do not labor or spin. Yet I tell you that not even Solomon in all his splendor was dressed like one of these. If that is how God clothes the grass of the field, which is here today and tomorrow is thrown into the fire, will he not much more clothe you, O you of little faith? So do not worry, saying, 'What shall we eat?' or 'What shall we drink?' or 'What shall we wear?' For the pagans run after all these things, and your heavenly Father knows that you need them. But seek first his kingdom and his righteousness, and all these things will be given to you as well. Therefore, do not worry about tomorrow, for tomorrow will worry about itself. Each day has enough trouble of its own."

The reference to daily bread addresses one of God's Great Promises: **God faithfully provides for His people.**

"Forgive us our sins." The Greek term for forgive is *afihmi*, which is a legal term, meaning to cancel or pardon a debt. A good example is found in Luke 7:41,

"Two men owed money to a certain moneylender. One owed him five hundred denarii, and the other fifty. Neither of them had the money to pay him back, so he canceled the debts of both."

Sin against anyone is first a sin against God because it is a transgression against the law of God to love one another.

"For we also forgive everyone who has wronged us." We must have the same unqualified forgiveness we received from Christ.

Matthew. 18:21&22
Then Peter came to Jesus and asked, "Lord, how many times shall I forgive my brother when he sins against me? Up to seven times?" Jesus answered, **"I tell you, not seven times, but seventy-seven times."**

Ephesians 4:32
Be kind and compassionate to one another, forgiving each other, just as in Christ God forgave you.

Matthew 6:14 &15
"For if you forgive men when they sin against you, your heavenly Father will also forgive you. But if you do not forgive men their sins, your Father will not forgive your sins."

"And lead us not into temptation," or "do not let us be led into temptation," or "deliver us from evil (Evil One)." All mean basically the same thing. We are asking God to protect us from the evil desires we all face and are tempted by. Each one has his own evil desires, and each one has his own limits of tolerance before he breaks and succumbs. God knows us intimately, as we pray for His protection for us individually. This truth addresses one of the Great Promises of God: **God faithfully protects His people.**

This prayer Jesus gave His disciples has deservedly received much attention over the years with much written about it, even whole books. It is a simple prayer, but like many of Jesus' sayings, it is laden with layers of meaning. It addresses the basics: God and His will first, His provision, His mercy, our mercy, and His protection. It is structured as a daily prayer. Early Christians prayed it three times a day.

Jesus continued to teach his disciples about prayer with a story. In His first example, it is important to note that the man does not turn his (apparently unexpected) visitor away, even though he is totally unprepared for visitors. That response would have violated mid-eastern hospitality customs. Instead, he went out into the darkness to find what was needed. He sacrificed his comfort and sleep to help another. He knew who his neighbor was and who could probably fill the need, so he went to him and asked him. The neighbor, however, first rebuffed him, trying to find out if this is a real need or just an intrusion. The key is that the man persisted, and the neighbor then gave him what he needed.

The persistence is illustrative of our trusting in God to provide for our needs. We know He can. Jesus is saying we need to persist in our petition, knowing all is possible with God, and He will provide what is needed, not only good things but also up to and including the Holy Spirit. Mature faith sees and believes God's promises, embracing them with persistence even though the answer does not come right away. Through the process of persistent prayer, we are forced to examine the nature of our requests, our motives for asking, and God's part in our prayers. It also makes us sift through our petitions and separate our wants from our needs. Persistent prayer develops and strengthens our relationship with God and provides us with specific answers to specific needs, all of which leads to testimony and praise. God will provide the best answer in the best time. Again, showing one of God's Great Promises: **God faithfully provides for His people**.

Jesus was then confronted by those who said he cast out demons because He used power given him by Beelzebub, the prince of demons. Others, having just witnessed Jesus drive out a demon from a mute who then spoke, asked for a sign—blind to the miracle they had just seen. Their logic did not stand. Jesus adroitly pointed out several key truths:

If Satan were a house divided, how could he stand?

One must be careful accusing Jesus of using Beelzebub's power because their people were doing the same thing. But, "if by the finger of God," as Jesus put it (NIV), then God's Kingdom was already here. Indeed, the Kingdom had come, in the very person of Jesus, though they did not understand.

In verses 21 & 22, Jesus' reference to the stronger man is to Himself who overcomes Satan and his demons, not by using Satan's power but by overpowering Satan Himself. The next illustration shows the absolute necessity of putting God in one's life after cleansing, not just superficially decorating to make everything look nice to everyone else. Without Him, the person is open to being re-infested with evil even worse than before.

The woman shouting out the blessing on Jesus meant only the best, a good Jewish blessing. Jesus, always looking to focus the crowd on the most important element at hand, redirected the blessing to hearing and obeying the word of God, much like the incident with Mary and Martha. They were hearing the word of God in a new and fresh way with great authority, and they were excited about it, but Jesus knew that without obedience all would be lost.

Luke, the master storyteller, casually introduces the next section by telling us the crowds greatly increased in size. As Jesus received more public attention, He made a rather startling announcement that they were a wicked generation, "These are evil times in which we live." Indeed, many had asked Him for signs but not for pure motives, so they were given none. They would someday be given the sign of Jonah: "as Jonah was to the Ninevites." Whatever Jonah's appearance and message were, when he finally reached Nineveh, they were incredibly effective. This citadel of a hostile enemy, the Assyrian Empire, repented to the LORD completely. They all turned humbly to God. For Jesus to be the same for everyone would cause them all to repent and turn to God. Many take this reference simply to mean the three days Jonah spent in the fish and was released was a foreshadowing of Jesus' rising on the third day from the tomb. Though this superficial similarity may also have been implied, Jesus was often not content to leave messages suffice on the surface. There was most often a deeper meaning. Repentance and humility are the higher agenda.

To illustrate his point, in verse 31 Jesus used the Queen of Sheba (Queen of the South), a Gentile, who recognized Solomon's wisdom. To say someone greater than Solomon was there would shock his listeners. Solomon was held to be the greatest of Israelite kings in terms of wisdom and wealth. The temple he built was the most magnificent in the world. Greater than Jonah? Someone who single-handedly "conquered" the Assyrians for the LORD? Yes, indeed. Far greater. This hard-to-believe attitude forecasted the way in which the gospel was later accepted: more readily among the Gentiles than among the Jews.

Jesus often used light to refer to the truth. No one who knows the truth, the good news, should hide it. Rather, they should display it for all to see. "Those who come in may see the light…" (verse 33). The eye, on the other hand, lets light into the body, so when the eyes are good, light streams in. If the eyes are not good, if they are clouded by prejudice and sin, then light cannot penetrate, thus their eyes are bad. Jesus went a step further and told them to keep their whole body full of light. Let no part escape the truth, leave no "dirty secrets" covered. Instead, cleanse the whole body, and light will permeate it all. Let truth completely light you and your way. This illustration points to those who accept Jesus' message. Darkness colors those who do not.

Jesus' teaching was fascinating and intriguing to a certain Pharisee, who invited Jesus to eat with him. Jesus very intentionally did not follow the custom of washing before dinner so He could offer a teaching moment. This Pharisee was probably very sorry he invited Jesus into his house! With this audience, Jesus took the opportunity to pronounce six condemnations against the Pharisees and the legal experts.

Jesus addressed them as fools, a strong term, used often in Hebrew scripture for those who ignored God's law and commandments or those who thought they knew better than God what was best. Though they strictly followed their rituals of cleaning their hands (and forearms and elbows), Jesus declared they were full of wickedness and greed. What they should have been doing was giving to the poor, from the heart, which would help put them in right relationship with God, making them pure.

But Jesus didn't stop there. He was just getting on a roll. He took full advantage of the opportunity to unload on the Pharisees and make them face the brutal truth of their hypocrisy. Instead of benefiting from all their perceived holy practices that they tried so hard for everyone to see, they were righteous only superficially, and their hearts were not in alignment with God's will.

How terrible judgment would be for the Pharisees! They were tithing in various ways, but ignoring the most important core of the faith: justice and the love of God.

> Micah 6:8
> He has shown you, O mortal, what is good.
> And what does the Lord require of you?
> To act justly and to love mercy
> and to walk humbly with your God.

The Pharisees thrived on the adoration of the public, selfishly taking the most esteemed places in public events. Jesus even compared them to unmarked graves. To touch a grave would make one unclean, so graves were always well marked in white, and people avoided them. Jesus was saying the Pharisees were so corrupt that if someone touched them they would be unclean. Not only were they not marked as graves, but also they were camouflaged in fine clothing! Consequently, they actually led people to become unclean.

This rebuke was too much for one of the legal experts in the room, not at all what he expected. He tried to interject a strong but polite message that these statements just might offend those in the room, including the legal experts. Instead of offering an apology, however, Jesus turned His wrath on the legal experts.

The scholars were admonished for creating so many rules that the people couldn't bear them all and then were doing nothing to help them know these rules or how to live with them.

Next, Jesus took on the hypocrisy of the Jewish leaders and their history with God's prophets, many of whom they had killed. Later tombs had been built to honor those who had been killed. They didn't follow the prophets' teachings while they were alive or after they were dead. God's plan, Jesus told them, included sending them more prophets and apostles, which they would both kill and prosecute, a prophecy about the early church and His own death. Therefore, this generation of Jewish leaders would bear the burden of all prior generations from Abel (considered the first prophet slain) to Zechariah (considered the last prophet slain, in the order of the Hebrew Scripture).

Jesus saved the most condemning word for last. The experts in the law were charged with teaching the people about the Law. According to Jesus, not only did they not use their knowledge to comprehend the Law fully; but also they did not pass along what they did know to the people. What a failure! Knowledge was highly revered in Jewish life and scripture. For those given the responsibility of understanding God's Law and teaching it to fail at both was a most damning indictment.

It is no wonder then that once Jesus left, the Pharisees and Scribes started to form an opposition against Him and make plans to trap Him and stop His ministry.

CHAPTER TWELVE

J esus was now drawing huge crowds, many thousands. He first took
His disciples aside and talked with them. He had just openly criticized
the Pharisees and warned His followers to be careful when dealing
with them. Their poison, which He openly named hypocrisy, was like
yeast. A little bit could permeate throughout the group.

And He quietly told them a startling revelation. All things will be
made known. All secrets will be revealed. Truth will prevail when
everything is exposed.

1 Corinthians 4:5
Therefore, judge nothing before the appointed time; wait till the
Lord comes. He will bring to light what is hidden in darkness and
will expose the motives of men's hearts. At that time each will receive his praise from God.

Ecclesiastes 12:14
For God will bring every deed into judgment, including every hidden thing, whether it is good or evil.

Jesus knew His church would suffer persecution, so He started to prepare His disciples. This represents one more of the Great Promises of God:
He faithfully prepares His people for what is to come. (When
Jesus begins or ends what he says with "I tell you," or "He who has ears
let him hear," then it is very important indeed.) Only God can send
peoples' souls to hell, so their fear should be limited to God alone, who

has control over their eternal destiny. Even though the small birds were cheap and used for temple sacrifices by the poor, God knew every one of them. The hairs of the disciples' heads were numbered? What a shocking concept for these followers of Jesus. He kept telling them about a God in a way they never before comprehended. God knew every detail about them, and they were valuable to God.

The next few statements are important to take together and in context. Jesus carefully laid down some very basic principles.

Those who declare "Jesus is Lord" will be acknowledged by Jesus in His role as the Son of Man, the agent of judgment, to the heavenly hosts. Those who disown Jesus, those who hear the truth of the gospel and do not accept it, those who reject Jesus as God's Son will be disowned by Jesus, as the Son of Man, to the heavenly hosts.

Everyone who spoke a word against the Son of Man would be forgiven. Everyone. Why? Because of their ignorance. They must not know Him, or they would not speak against Him. If they understood His true nature, they would accept Him, so God would forgive them out of the eternal abundance of His great mercy.

But anyone who blasphemed or insulted the Holy Spirit would not be forgiven. This was the one unforgivable sin. Why? Because in doing so the person had separated himself from the very One who made it possible to attain forgiveness. Humanity cannot bridge that gap through its own power. For example, these followers would not be able to withstand the pending persecution on their own without the power of the Holy Spirit. To attempt to stand firm on their own was to push the Holy Spirit away, to grieve the Holy Spirit, and to segregate oneself from His power.

This core principle should remind us all of original sin which separated us from God when we think we can sustain ourselves without God or at least whenever we feel like it. If we believe this, we do so at our peril.

Verses 11 and 12 are often taken out of context. Here Jesus was clearly addressing the time when his followers would be persecuted and brought before the authorities. Again, He was stressing the need for them to rely on the Holy Spirit and not themselves in these situations. The Holy Spirit is the spirit of truth and by relying on Him, the truth would be told in those venues, which was part of God's plan.

Jesus prepared His disciples for the consequences of bearing His message, telling them not to be afraid of men and to trust God.

Sensing a pause in the dialogue, someone in the crowd blurted out what's been burning in his mind—money. Jesus was obviously totally put off by the interjection. "Sounds like you are concerned with greed, so let's make this a teachable moment about greed. Life is not about stuff!" Wow! Really? Tell that to most 21st century Moderns. We're in trouble!

Jesus shared the parable about the Rich Fool. The rich man scored a great harvest. His reaction? How to hog it all for himself and live off of it. The word "I" is used six times in the story. God's reaction to that plan? "You fool!" Strong words from the Ultimate Source. The Giver of Life is about to take the man's life away. God gives abundantly so it can be shared with those in need.

> Proverbs 22:9
> The generous will themselves be blessed,
> for they share their food with the poor.

> Matthew 10:8b
> Freely you have received; freely give.

Jesus then turned back to his disciples to teach about life's worries. People naturally worry about all kinds of things, like what to eat, what to wear, and so forth, but Jesus said don't. God provides. He provides for the things in nature; He will provide for you because you are much more valuable than all those in nature. Worry provides nothing. The pagan world does worry about these things, obsesses about these things. God knows what you need, and He will provide. Seek God! He will provide! Get your priorities right. God first and the rest will fall into place. Trust God.

Here again we see one of the Great Promises of God. Just as He always prepares His people for what is to come, **God faithfully provides for His people.**

Possessions are not needed for sustenance. God has given everything to humanity. He is eager to give to those who ask. Those who are rich should share with those who are poor and disadvantaged. Jesus hit the nail on the head, the truth of humanity, the tie of money and heart in verse 34:

"For where your treasure is, there your heart will be also."

As He is quoted in the Gospel of Matthew:

Matthew 6:24b
"You cannot serve both God and Money."

Matthew put this quotation right before his version of the discourse about "do not worry"

Jesus then turned to being prepared, using terms and scenes familiar to them. The New King James translation says, "waist be girded," meaning pull the hem of the robe up and tucked into the waist, ready to run—the picture of readiness. The modern equivalent might be "rolling up your sleeves," ready for work. Most other translations segue more neatly into the wedding scenario. Putting themselves in the place of servants, waiting for their master to come back from a wedding banquet sets the stage. Weddings were very special occasions, and the groom was treated like a king on his wedding day. Anything he wanted that was possible was done to make that day memorable. These servants would be ready at the blink of an eye to jump up when he came to the door. It's that kind of anticipation Jesus was telling them they should maintain in waiting for Him to return: dressed and ready to serve. The reward will be good for those who are ready.

Jesus turned the story around. When He finally shows up, late in the night, He will have them recline at the table, and He will serve them. But they must be ready. Why? Because "The Son of Man will come at an hour when you do not expect him." So much for all the prognostication about when Jesus will return! When will He? When we least expect it! So we must be ready at all times and at any time.

Peter, seeking some clarification and knowing they were hearing eternal truths from God's son, asked if He was sharing insider information.

However, he did not get a direct answer; instead, Jesus continued to teach.

Wise and prudent slaves who had proved their abilities became managers for their master, operating the estate much like a business manager. They were entrusted with funds, had hiring and firing authority, and represented the master on most matters of everyday operation of the household. This manager is the profile Jesus used here. If he were performing his duties when the master returns, life would be good for him. If, however, he became corrupted by his position of power and took advantage of his authority, abusing the other slaves, upon the return of the master, he would be severely punished, and "assigned a place with the unbelievers" (Matthew 12:46 NIV).

From this extreme case, Jesus moved to two other examples of obedience. First was the servant who knew what was supposed to be done and did not do it. He would be punished. Second was the servant who did not know what was supposed to be done. He also did not do the right thing, but he was punished less because he did not know better. The more one has been entrusted with the more is demanded of that person. As James put it in his letter:

> James 3:1
> Not many of you should become teachers, my fellow believers,
> because you know that we who teach will be judged more strictly.

Jesus then turned to the big picture. Bringing fire upon the earth is to purify it and judge the people. The disciples hearing Jesus speak would immediately conjure up images of the prophets of old and their fiery prophesies, especially about the Day of the LORD. The Holy Spirit was also often associated with fire (i.e. Pentecost and other instances where people became believers in Acts), and it was with fire that God's plan worked in John's Revelation. Jesus was eager for that process to begin. He first must endure the suffering of the torture of the Romans and the crucifixion itself. This is the baptism to which He was referring. Once He went through it, He would rise out of it a new creation, the Glorified Christ.

The common understanding of the Messiah was that after disposing of the occupying military force, there would be a kingdom of peace on earth. Jesus addressed this misperception, saying He was not there to bring peace on earth, rather division. All the divisiveness He cited would happen as a result of individual decisions made when people were faced with the truth of the gospel. Indeed, families would be torn apart by these decisions.

Jesus turned to the crowd and referenced some common sense weather truisms. His point was that the truth of what was right before them, the Son of God in the flesh, evaded them. The word he uses for "hypocrites" has in Hebrew the root meaning "godless" (without a god base). He then encourages them to make up their own minds. By now, they should be able to see the facts for what they are. They have been presented with the truth. All must face judgment. Better to reconcile, repent, and accept Christ before it is too late than to suffer the consequences of rejecting Him.

CHAPTER THIRTEEN

A s He made His way to Jerusalem, Jesus was trying very hard, with His own sense of urgency, to teach as much as He could at every opportunity. Someone in the crowd referred to an incident about Pilate's men killing some Jews in the temple who were making sacrifices. Such an abomination! They must have been guilty of great sins to have died such deaths! The commonly held belief was that if one died or suffered terribly, it was because that person had committed serious sin(s). For example, the story in John:

John 9:1&2
As he went along, he saw a man blind from birth.
His disciples asked him, "Rabbi, who sinned, this man or his parents, that he was born blind?"

But Jesus said, "No!" Then he admonished them to repent themselves, or they would perish. In other words, just because this belief you have had all these years is not true, it does not free you to go out and sin without risking judgment. As Paul later put it:

Romans 6:1&2
What shall we say, then? Shall we go on sinning so that grace may increase? By no means!

Likewise, Jesus pointed out, those killed when a tower collapsed (verse 4) were not guiltier than others. It was an accident, not an act of judgment. All are sinners.

> Romans 3:23
> For all have sinned and fall short of the glory of God,

> Ecclesiastes 7:20
> There is not a righteous man on earth who does what is right and never sins.

> Psalms 143:2b
> no one living is righteous before you.

> Psalms 14:3
> All have turned aside, they have together become corrupt; there is no one who does good, not even one.

Everyone needed to repent or risk losing eternal life. To help make the point, Jesus told them the parable of the fig tree.

The fig tree was at least three years old. If it was planted three years ago, then this would be the year one could expect it to bear fruit, especially if it were grown in a vineyard. The owner of the vineyard had good reason to cut it down if it was bare, but the vineyard keeper asked the owner for one more year, one more chance to make a difference. The people were being given one more chance to repent. The fig tree was being used to represent the Jewish people, again. The prophets had used the same metaphor; now, Jesus used it in a simple illustration. What the people did not know is that Jesus was the keeper of the vineyard; He who was asking the master, Father God, for another chance for the people; He stood between them and the ax. It is a good illustration of both the mercy of God, granting an additional year, a reprieve to allow for repentance; but also it shows the ultimate, inevitable judgment of God.

On this trip to Jerusalem, Jesus continued to visit the synagogue on the Sabbath wherever He was and teach. We don't know in what town He was for the next scene, but He was always on the lookout for opportunities to heal. From within the synagogue He saw a certain woman, which means He would have had to see her beyond the slatted partition between the main room and the segregated room for women. She had been crippled for 18 years, implying she had not always been that way. She could not stand erect, something which differentiated humans from animals, so she maintained a demeaning posture at all times, negatively reinforcing her disadvantage of being a woman. Before she said anything, Jesus called her to the front.

Isaiah 65:24
"Before they call, I will answer."

The woman didn't say anything. Jesus simply healed her by laying His hands on her. Immediately, she stood straight and praised God. A simple act of Jesus with a miraculous result. Though she could not lift herself, Christ lifted her up.

Psalms 146:8
The LORD gives sight to the blind
The LORD lifts up those who are bowed down,
The LORD loves the righteous.

You would expect everyone there to rejoice with this woman, but the leader of the synagogue did not. Instead, he reprimanded the people for seeking healing on the Sabbath. Jesus rebutted him by pointing out that people take their livestock out for a drink of water on the Sabbath, which was even allowed within the Law. If one could give a poor animal some water, then surely a person who had been suffering for eighteen years could be healed on the Sabbath! By framing his response in the context of Satan, Jesus brings the message: "How would you like to be bound by Satan's demons for eighteen years?" The animals could be untied, set free, but the woman could not? He called them hypocrites. These legalists were so shackled by the details of the Law that they could not see the purpose for which it was written, including the Sabbath. They were bound by the Law but were blind to the truth of the coming of the Kingdom of God, which would free souls.

Jesus' rebuttal struck home. The leader and his associates were humiliated, and the people were delighted.

Jesus, having everyone's attention, took the opportunity to teach about the Kingdom of God. His first illustration was the mustard seed, which is a very small seed. "A man" is a generic term, the same as "Adam" or "the first man." Trees were often used in stories to represent nations. This tree grew large. "Birds of the air" implied very numerous, so the tree would have to be quite big. The tree could represent the Church.

His second example was yeast, which when added to the flour, works its way through all the dough. He referred to a large amount of flour to make his point—roughly sixty pounds. Yeast makes things grow from the inside; it permeates the whole. It could represent the Holy Spirit.

One conversation Luke thought important to include as Jesus traveled toward Jerusalem centered on a question someone asked along the way. "Lord, will only a few be saved?" A difficult question, no doubt. It was probably based on the commonly held belief that only the Jews would be saved.

Side note: There is also the history of the remnant. Time and time again in the Jewish history, when the people were overcome by outside powers, taken away as slaves, or divided by internal warfare, there would remain a remnant of God's people. The remnant may have been just a small group, isolated from the others, or it may have been a small number of people dispersed with pure hearts, remaining true to God in the midst of trial. God always seemed to keep a remnant and use it to regenerate his people.

Jesus' response was to "make every effort" to enter through the narrow door. "Strive" in other translations has the same root word as agony, implying a continuous process, never letting up, giving it your all. Following Jesus' way in this world would not easy. To do so continuously with strong effort would be difficult.

2 Timothy 4:7
I have fought the good fight, I have finished the race, I have kept
the faith.

Those that tried and could not were those who attempted to gain salvation on their own. There would be a time when the door would close.
Those not inside will be cut off. There will be a time of judgment. If the
master does not know them, if they do not have a personal relationship
with Christ, it will then be too late. Where they come from will be
irrelevant and genealogy not important. Just being a Jew will not be
sufficient. "You were one of us" will not hold any sway. Mere association
will not count. The true core of Jewish heritage, Abraham, Isaac, and
Jacob will be inside, as well as the prophets. Those who came from all
over the world, meaning Gentiles, will be inside. Yes, indeed, the world
will be turned upside down. The people needed to understand that
salvation and judgment could not be separated.

Jesus' path had apparently taken Him into Perea, which was controlled
by Herod. Some Pharisees came to Him and warned Him that Herod
wanted to kill Him and that He should leave the area. Most likely they
just would have liked for Jesus to leave the area. Jesus showed no respect
for Herod, the killer of John the Baptist, calling him a fox. His plan was
to follow God's plan, which would not be thwarted. His plan included
driving out demons and healing people. The timeline as stated in verse 33
is relatively indefinite in Aramaic but with a conclusion; usually a short
time. It was a colloquialism used often.

Hosea 6:2
After two days, he will revive us; on the third day he will restore us,
that we may live in his presence.

This "third day" reference also reminds us of Jonah. Jesus added that
He must get to Jerusalem because that's where all the prophets met their
doom.

The mention of the name of the City of David struck a strong emo-
tional chord in Jesus. The city had played a critical part in the history of

Israel, especially with the temple, which formerly housed the Ark of the Covenant, with the very Presence of God. Indeed, many prophets had spoken God's word in Jerusalem only to be killed for the truth. Christ, the Author of Life, longed to cradle the city in His arms and heal it, but the people resisted endlessly. He mourned the city, its house desolate—the temple was empty, the Ark was gone, the Presence of the LORD had left. Yet He foretold the triumphal entry He would make which would begin His last week, leading up to the crucifixion, quoting from Psalm 118.

CHAPTER FOURTEEN

L uke sets the stage for the next scene with some explosive material. It's a Sabbath. Jesus was at the house of one of the leaders of the Pharisees. At this point, they were watching everything He did to see if He "made a mistake." A man with abnormal swelling of the body was there. What a powder keg! You have to wonder how he got there. Was he a plant by the Pharisees and legal experts to see what Jesus would do?

Jesus lit the fuse by asking, "Does the Law allow healing on the Sabbath or not?" Plain and simple, yes or no, but He got no response. Jesus took hold of the man, healed him, and sent him away. He then cited an example from the Law (Deut. 5:14), asking if saving a son or an ox that fell down a well were not acceptable on the Sabbath. Again, no response. The obvious answer would have to be yes (because at its root, the Law is merciful), but that answer would have led to an awkward question they did not want to confront.

Jesus, ever the observant guest, watched the way the socially conscious Pharisees seated themselves around the table, looking for the most prestigious places. His parable is rather transparent. It's not really a parable, but a lesson in humility rewarded. The setting of a wedding is really the only element that politely separated it from the current affair. (It is, however, interesting that the wedding theme is used here, shortly before Jesus spoke about the Great Banquet.) This theme of the exalted being humbled and the meek being edified is prevalent throughout Luke. It is one of the many lessons Jesus taught that appeared to turn the world's thinking on its head and definitely challenged the social norm then and even now. It was not, however, a new lesson.

Proverbs 25:6 & 7
Do not exalt yourself in the king's presence,
and do not claim a place among great men;
it is better for him to say to you, "Come up here,"
than for him to humiliate you before a nobleman.

Jesus commanded the attention of the room and continued to teach. Reciprocity should not be the governing rule for inviting guests to eat. Instead, one should bring in those who cannot repay, not in search for a reward but out of love and sharing one's blessings. One will be blessed not only by those who come but also by God.

Apparently one person was really trying to understand what Jesus was saying. Well versed in Hebrew scripture and tradition, he spoke about a feast in the Kingdom of God, which was to occur in the Messianic Age. Jesus ignored the comment but took the theme of a banquet to launch into another parable.

A great banquet was to be held for many guests. They were notified, but when it came time for the banquet, they all had some lame excuse why they were not going to be there. Who buys a field without looking at it? Who buys an oxen team without trying it first? Who plans their wedding at the same time as the banquet if they really plan on going? So the host of the banquet reached out to the disenfranchised. There was still room for more. Then he reached out to anyone who would listen. Those who were first invited, though, were not allowed in.

Salvation was first offered to the Pharisees and Scribes but was rejected. They should have been the first to recognize Jesus for who He was, but they rejected Him. The blessing was then offered to the common people, the socially rejected, the uneducated, and many accepted it; they accepted Jesus. Later salvation was extended to the Gentiles, who embraced it.

Jesus taught the crowds differently than He taught His disciples. The crowds received more oblique parables, which they had to work out themselves. Sometimes, Jesus said things to the crowds that shocked them, and He would leave them dangling, pondering what He meant. His methods were, of course, intentional. The people talked among themselves. The Holy Spirit was at work then and later after Jesus was resurrected. Later, in retrospect, some of the puzzling sayings were more understandable and served to act as fertile soil for the teaching of the apostles.

As Jesus got closer to Jerusalem, the crowds were getting larger. Not only is His following becoming quite popular, but also this was time for folks to start making their way to Jerusalem for the Passover. Jesus was never interested in the size of His following. He was much more concerned with their understanding the personal sacrifice necessary to be a true disciple.

Jesus confronted the ever increasing crowd with the requirements of being one of His disciples, the true meaning of discipleship. He made it abundantly clear that their commitment must be to Him first, above all others, including oneself. To take up one's cross was to march to one's death. Jesus was telling them they must give up everything they love for Him. He must be first. If they truly understood, they would know He was really restating the Shema and applying it to Himself:

Deuteronomy 6:5
Love the Lord your God with all your heart and with all your soul
and with all your strength.

This is the essence of what God wants, for He wants all to be saved (1 Tim 2:3): to surrender all allegiances and give all to God. The giving of one's self is the hardest. We moderns have the most difficulty with this concept. We have been brought up being taught in the power of the individual; everything in our society is built around the individual, even relationships. Yet we are to take our dreams, wants, needs, things we hold most dear and push them aside, holding Jesus up as our first love and only commitment. For, as he told us:

Luke 12:31
"Seek his kingdom, and these things will be given to you as well."

For Jesus, the cross was a symbol of God's will. This is why Jesus came: to die. This was the will of God: that Jesus would die for the sins of the world. Did He not accept it, saying "Yet not as I will, but as You will"? In this text, Jesus is telling each disciple that he must take up his cross daily. They had

Side note: When a criminal was to be crucified, he was forced to carry the cross-beam through the city to the place of crucifixion. This act demonstrated to all his submission/obedience to the authority against which he had rebelled. He was submitting to Rome's will.

to make the same decision Jesus made: to accept the will of God for their lives, daily, whatever or wherever God's will may lead them. We submit to God's will. Submission leading to death—the death of the old self. Likewise, it leads to life—life eternal with God, starting with the initial obedience of submission.

This sacrifice does not mean stoically facing life's troubles, as it has become to mean in the secular world. ("I have my crosses to bear.") Rather, it is obedience to God's will as revealed in His word, accepting the consequences without reservation for Jesus' sake and the gospel. These consequences can range from embarrassment to discomfort to suffering and death.

The sub-theme of "daily" in Luke surfaces here again. As in the manna, God rejuvenates us and our relationship with Him every day. Jesus teaches about taking each day on its own. His prayer teaches us to ask for our daily bread. Here he tells us to take up our cross daily: to accept the will of our Father daily. Each day ask for His will and be obedient to it. His Spirit will enable you. There is no joy greater than doing His will. Your faith will grow. You will grow closer to God. Each day.

The example of building a tower is simple. What is desired to be for fame quickly becomes shame when it is left half completed because it was not well planned. The example of going to war is hyperbolical to make a similar point. This decision to become Jesus' disciple is not one to make without considerable thought and planning. It really is an all-or-nothing commitment and a life and death decision. Christ is the Author of Life. All life was created through him and continues because of him.

Jesus is not looking for naïve, simplistic followers who love Him because He can heal them or because He speaks words of peace and comfort. He is looking for disciples who will wholly commit themselves to Him, surrender themselves to Him, depend on Him, and trust in Him.

Matthew 19:27
Peter answered him, "We have left everything to follow you! What then will there be for us? "

Matthew 19:29
Jesus said to them, **"And everyone who has left houses or brothers or sisters or father or mother or wife or children or fields for my sake will receive a hundred times as much and will inherit eternal life."**

This commitment was not something that could be done alone.

Zechariah 4:6b
'Not by might nor by power, but by my Spirit,' says the LORD Almighty.

It requires the power of the Holy Spirit. But more on that later. Luke leaves this powerful, life-changing section with Jesus telling the crowd that those who are listening really need to remember this teaching.

CHAPTER FIFTEEN

C hapter Fifteen, as the gospel is now divided, is composed of three parables of items being lost: a sheep, a coin, and a son. Jesus taught these stories, no doubt, many times along the way, and Luke carefully arranges them here. He starts with setting the scene with the Pharisees and legal experts watching Jesus teach, surrounding Himself with "sinners," such as tax collectors and others not named.

In the first parable, Jesus makes it personal. Instead of talking about "a man," he personalizes it by using "you." Sheep do not intentionally run away. They just aren't too smart. They get easily attracted to little things and end up wandering off.

Isaiah 53:6
We all, like sheep, have gone astray, each of us has turned to his own way;

The thing is, sheep cannot take care of themselves, and they cannot find their own way back. They are defenseless and vulnerable to predators. Out of concern, the shepherd went himself to search for the one sheep. The others were safe in their group, probably with a younger shepherd. The head shepherd rejoiced when he found it.

Then he spread the good news, and a there was celebration. Jesus compared this story to the salvation of a person and the subsequent rejoicing in heaven every time one of the lost was found. It's not that the ninety-nine weren't important, but finding the lost one was reason for celebration. There had been rejoicing when each of the ninety-nine were saved as well.

There is another layer to this parable, however, just like many Jesus told. It is a story about evangelism. We know, with ninety-nine sheep, we are missing one. We must leave the "open country" and go after the lost sheep until we find it. Then we take up its burdens and help it home. It is a persistent search by a responsible shepherd. Even though we are tired from the search, the success is shared with others, and there is joy, just like the joy that inevitably occurs when salvation is found in Luke's book of Acts. Joy as one comes to God; joy for the helper, for the angels, for God. This joy **must** be part of heaven! If the joy for one lost sheep is that great on earth, imagine what joy must exist in heaven itself!

Contrast the joy Jesus tells about with the attitude of the Pharisees.

The woman in Jesus' next story has ten coins. Because Luke wrote in Greek, the coins are called drachmas, each worth about a day's wages. These could very possibly have been part of her marriage headdress (what women wore on their forehead on their wedding day and after). So valued were these coins that they could not be taken from her, even for the payment of a debt. In the story she was missing one of the coins, making the headdress incomplete. Her search was intense, persistent. As a result, she found it. Again the focused, personal effort paid off. The joy was shared with those she cared about—her friends and neighbors, and there was a celebration. Again, Jesus compares this joy to the joy in heaven over one sinner who repents.

In light of their respective opening verses, these first two parables must be seen together. It was the Pharisees' exclusivity that stimulates Jesus' telling of the stories, and set against the Pharisees' prejudice that, He illustrates God's love for all. His love was not for just "the elect" (the Jews or Jews that obey the Law). Both parables teach that God actually goes out and seeks the lost. He doesn't wait for them to come groveling at His feet.

The two stories do a good job of illustrating the difference between the Old Covenant and what it had become, with all the man-made regulations added onto the Law, taking the laws to their logical extreme and distorting it so it could not even function in the way for which it had been created. God's Word had been so polluted that it was barely recognizable. Then the Pharisees used this distorted hybrid to judge the people.

The third story is, of course, the most famous of all. It is found only in Luke, where he very intentionally couples it with the pair of other lost parables. But this story is so much more.

The man was blessed. He had two sons. The elder was entitled to a double portion of the estate, which in this case would be two-thirds; the younger would receive one-third. All this would be distributed to the sons upon the father's death. For the son to ask for his inheritance early was highly irregular and socially inappropriate, but the father complied. The son would receive the value at the time but no future earnings, so it is very similar to withdrawing one's retirement funds from their investments and liquidating them to cash. It was a foolish move. It even showed a lack of respect for his father, yet the father went along with it. The son had the freedom to make mistakes, just as humanity has freedom of choice and often makes mistakes.

In this case, the son took what he received from his father and left for a distant country, somewhere that his father could not watch over him or tell him what to do or how to do it. He would be totally free to do what he pleased with his money. So what did he do there? He wasted all his money by living extravagantly. He lived recklessly, without rules. At home, there had been rules, God's rules, taught and enforced by his father. Here he found that living without those rules ruined him. The rules had been for his best interest, much like the Law acted to protect the Hebrews, and when they rebelled, they suffered.

At the same time his money ran out, there was a severe famine in that country. No one had any extra food or resources to share. Totally destitute and desperate, he begged for work and ended up doing a job any Jew would avoid if possible—feeding pigs. Not only was it a nasty job, but also pigs were unclean to Jews. He couldn't even eat the pig food, and there was no other food to spare. The pigs got what they needed, but he got nothing.

One day, he "came to his senses." The dream he had chased had become a nightmare, and reality hit hard. Repentance begins by seeing things as they are. Before, he was running away—away from his father, away from God. He was not himself but a character in his own play. Now, by the conviction of reality, he "came to himself." His father's slaves had what they needed, plenty in fact. "I will…" (Verse 18). A statement of fact, an emphatic act of will, a conscious decision, not just wishful thinking.

Part of his plan was a confession to his father, absolutely necessary for repentance. He had sinned against heaven by disobeying his father, tricking him, and not honoring him. He had sinned against his father. This admission was a personal level of acknowledgement. It is one thing to accept one's global sin and in concept, quite another to personalize it, especially against one's parent. He determined to admit his state, that he was no longer worthy to be called his father's son, and he was willing to humble himself and take on the role of a servant. With this plan firmly in his heart and his mind, he headed home.

Yes, the son had a plan, a good plan, as he headed home. While he was still a "long way off," his father saw him. He had always been watching, waiting, and when he saw his son, he was filled with compassion. He didn't wait for him to arrive. He ran to meet him and gave him an uninhibited embrace and kiss. Surely, this display of affection shocked the son, yet to his credit, he still blurted out what he had practiced in his mind so many times. His father ignored his words.

The father interrupted the rest of the son's speech. There were more important matters at hand. "Quick!" All these things must be done and done quickly. The page must be turned. The son that was dead was alive again; he had been lost and was found. Put a robe on him, to honor him. Put a ring on his hand, to show he had authority—he is family. Put sandals on his feet, for he was not a slave (they went barefoot). The fatted calf, reserved for the most auspicious of occasions, was to be prepared. Celebration!

The instructions from the father aroused excitement and all was wonderful except to the elder son, who had been out in the field working, being the good, dutiful son he was. He came home at the end of a hard day and heard all the celebration and then found out why. Instead of being happy about his brother's safe return home and joining the celebration, he refused to go in and participate. The father came out, meeting him where he was and tried to reason with him. The son pleaded, "I have obeyed the rules. I haven't sinned. I have performed good works." Notice he is basically saying that he had been "slaving" all these years, yet when he refers to his brother, he can't bring himself to say "brother;" instead, he says, "this son of yours who has squandered your property with prostitutes…"

Wisely the father replied to his elder son with love, "You are always with me, and everything I have is yours." This was very true. He stood to inherit everything because the younger son had already taken his inheritance. Everything had always been at his disposal really, he just hadn't asked. He felt he had to earn it.

There are and have been so many interpretations of this story. Most of them center on the older brother representing the self-righteous Pharisees, demanding God's approval based on their good works. They resent grace being given to sinners, failing to see they are also sinners. But God sees the heart. He doesn't judge like the elder son. As God rejoices in the salvation of the individual, so should the Pharisees rejoice in the salvation of "sinners."

The other aspect worth considering is that, like many of Jesus' other parables, this story must be taken personally. We can all probably understand demanding something from God and actually getting it, only to squander it. We receive it and leave God's presence for a while, pursuing our own agenda, ignoring His rules, and eventually suffering the consequences. Only then do we realize those rules were given to us to protect us, if only from ourselves. We find ourselves far off the path and begging God to forgive us and accept us back.

The one thing of which we can all be assured is that God never loses sight of us. He, through the grace of Jesus Christ, is eager for our return. God is always ready with unconditional mercy for any who ask, any who are willing to acknowledge their sinful state, and any who humble themselves, any who readily confess and then submit to God's perfect love. This is grace. God gives us His **Great Promises** on which we can rely.

CHAPTER SIXTEEN

J esus was telling His disciples a parable about a prodigal manager. The manager for a rich man was a slave who had proven his trust to handle money and affairs, such as purchases and running the household in the owner's absence. He had full control. Apparently, the rich man received credible information which led him to doubt his manager's trustworthiness, so he called him in and demanded to see the books. Because there was some doubt, he would be dismissed. It was a zero-tolerance situation.

The manager's reaction was classic. He had dug himself quite a hole. Not only had he indebted himself by manipulating the owner's money, but also he had no contingency plan. He had no skills, and he had been living such a life style that he would be totally ashamed to beg. He had to come up with something that would provide him with some income. He was still manager while the audit was in progress, so he leveraged his position with the current vendors. He surmised that they would feel indebted to him if he cut them a better deal. Then, when he was no longer employed, they would be much more likely to help him out, maybe even give him some long-term "loans."

The master found out what the manager did with the vendors. There was a grudging respect for the manger's actions, and the master actually commended him for acting shrewdly. Obviously, these two men were cut from the same cloth.

The point, according to Jesus, is that the people who deal in worldly affairs are inherently shrewder than "people of the light." Jesus' disciples were in fact children of the light.

John 12:35&36

Then Jesus told them, **"You are going to have the light just a little while longer. Walk while you have the light, before darkness overtakes you. The man who walks in the dark does not know where he is going. Put your trust in the light while you have it, so that you may become sons of light."**

Ephesians 5:8

For you were once darkness, but now you are light in the Lord. Live as children of light

1 Thessalonians 5:5

You are all sons of the light and sons of the day.

But they were not shrewd. What should they do? They should use the gifts given them by God, the money they have, and spend it on those who would be welcoming them when they get to heaven.

Jesus goes on to tell them a great truth. If a person can be trusted with a little money, they can be trusted with much more. Likewise, if one cannot be trusted with a little, they cannot be trusted with more. People often think that if they have more money, they can solve their problems and work out any financial crises they may have. But the data clearly shows, as Dave Ramsey and others have researched, that those who spend more than they make continue to do so even if they increase their income substantially. If one cannot manage money, how can one handle spiritual gifts, the "true riches" to which Jesus is referring?

Jesus continued by applying the same principle to property. Property had a special place in the hearts of the Jews. All property was understood to belong to God, given to the people to act as stewards of the property on His behalf. Yes, they treated property as though they owned it, but there was a certain reverence about their caretaker role, so for Jesus to apply the analogy to property was to take the lesson to another level.

Speaking about property leads Jesus to put the dichotomy in stark contrast, especially for the Pharisees. "One cannot serve two masters." Simple statement. Most would readily agree. But then Jesus says, **"You cannot**

serve both God and money." You cannot be a servant/slave to both God and money. They are diametrically opposed. The first approach is to follow the Great Commandment: "Love the Lord your God with all your heart and with all your soul and with all your strength." (Deut. 6:4&5) The other follows the line of original sin, where personal agendas take precedence over God's. If one becomes a slave to money, it shows a lack of faith in God's provision. One's perception is so focused on himself and his abilities to "succeed" that God gets lost in the weeds. He may get a weekly nod, but it's a far cry from following with all your heart, and that's where Jesus turns next.

The Pharisees did not want to believe the truth Jesus was presenting. Their heritage taught that wealth came to those who deserved it as a reward from God, so what Jesus was saying not only made no sense but also would totally upset their world-view. It would also destroy the façade they had created for themselves and convinced the people to believe—that the Pharisees were high and holy people. But that mirage was all pride. God knew their hearts.

Jeremiah 17:10
"I the LORD search the heart..."

1Samuel 16:7
"Man looks at the outward appearance, but the LORD looks at the heart."

All the things the people had been taught were of value—riches, big houses, large stables, jewelry—were all selfish material possessions. It was the idolization of them that God detested, so much so that He included it in His 10 Commandments.

Knowing His time was short, Jesus continued to teach, trying to emphasize as many of the important concepts as possible and putting those truths in proper perspective. He started with the Law and the Prophets, which comprised the base of the Hebrew Scriptures. John the Baptist was the fulcrum upon which history turns. From John forward, the good news of the Kingdom of God is preached. It was being preached forcefully and being received enthusiastically. This teaching was the fulfillment of the Law and the predictions of the prophets. The Law, given by God, was sacred. Not the least stroke of the pen (serif) would disappear or be altered from the Law. The serif is the smallest stroke, the small accent mark above or below a letter, yet it can change the meaning of the letter.

To make His point, Jesus took one of the topics the legal scholars used for their discussions and brought it into focus. Divorce was very common. All a man had to do was write a document of divorce, present it to the elders, and it was done. Jesus told them that original marriage was sacred, and subsequent marriages were the same as adultery.

Jesus' next parable brought several of His basic principles together. He first introduced the rich man. He did so with an economy of words but painted a picture his audience would fully appreciate. Not only was he rich, which would automatically conjure up a stereotype, but he didn't even have to work, living in luxury every day. He dressed in the most expensive clothing possible: purple, usually reserved for royalty due to its cost and linen that was normally saved for special occasions.

The next character was a beggar, Lazarus, the only person in a parable to have a name. It is a shortened version of a name meaning "God has helped." He was laid at the rich man's gate, meaning he was so disabled he had to be put there by others. He was ill. He had the same condition Job had with exposed sores. Luke, being the physician, used the medical term of the day to describe the condition. All Lazarus wanted was to eat the crumbs that fell to the floor. When the rich cleaned their hands during a meal, they often used pieces of bread and crumbs would fall to the floor with food residue. This reference was used by the woman in Syria Phoenicia when she begged Jesus to save her daughter's life (Mt 15:27 and Mk 7:28). Lazarus was not crying but apparently quietly and patiently waiting. He was so weak he could not fend off the unclean dogs. Perhaps, the licking of his wounds would provide some soothing—more mercy than he received from the rich man.

The beggar died. God's angels took him to the "bosom of Abraham," the paradise of contentment where the righteous wait for their inevitable vindication. The image was of Lazarus reclining at a table, a banquet, next to Abraham.

The rich man too died.

Ecclesiastes 7:2b
death is the destiny of every man...

The rich man went to hell, the place of torment, where he would stay with the other wicked who have died until the final judgment. He saw Lazarus and Abraham far away, across a huge chasm. Was this vision part of the torture? Both men were aware of each other in the world and after death. Now, the rich man begged for mercy from Abraham, asking that Lazarus provide him relief. He begged more loudly than Lazarus ever did, begging for mercy that he did not deserve and asking that Lazarus be his servant.

Father Abraham did respond and called him "son," for all of the Jews are his children. (There are commentators who see Abraham in this parable representing Christ, to whom all judgment is given.) Abraham set the record straight. "You had it good on earth, and Lazarus didn't. Now you suffer, and Lazarus is comforted." The chasm between them was fixed. No one could cross it from either side. Eternal fate is just that, eternal. God's divine judgment is just and irrevocable.

The rich man took another tact. Still treating Lazarus like a servant, he asked Abraham to send him to his father's house to warn his brothers. Ah, but they already had the Law and the Prophets, they should know. They needed to hear it from someone from the dead. No, if they did not believe the truth found in the writings of the Prophets and Moses (the Law), then they would not believe even if someone rises from the dead. What imagery! What foretelling by Jesus! The Jews who were listening to this parable could not discern the truth of God's word from the scriptures, nor would they recognize it after Jesus' resurrection.

John 12:37-40
Even after Jesus had done all these miraculous signs in their presence, they still would not believe in him. This was to fulfill the word of Isaiah the prophet: "Lord, who has believed our message and to whom has the arm of the Lord been revealed?" For this

reason, they could not believe, because, as Isaiah says elsewhere: "He has blinded their eyes and deadened their hearts, so they can neither see with their eyes, nor understand with their hearts, nor turn—and I would heal them."

Even with signs and wonders, you have to be careful, because Satan will use these to distract many:

2 Thessalonians 2:9-10
The coming of the lawless one will be in accordance with the work of Satan displayed in all kinds of counterfeit miracles, signs, and wonders, and in every sort of evil that deceives those who are perishing. They perish because they refused to love the truth and so be saved.

Revelation 13:11-14
Then I saw another beast, coming out of the earth. He had two horns like a lamb, but he spoke like a dragon. He exercised all the authority of the first beast on his behalf, and made the earth and its inhabitants worship the first beast, whose fatal wound had been healed. And he performed great and miraculous signs, even causing fire to come down from heaven to earth in full view of men. Because of the signs he was given power to do on behalf of the first beast, he deceived the inhabitants of the earth.

Jesus did in fact rise from the dead (Hallelujah!), but this reality did not immediately yield a crowd of converts. Even the raising of the other Lazarus didn't stimulate repentance, but rather plots to kill both Jesus and Lazarus.

The Pharisees would have supposed the rich man to be righteous and Lazarus to be a sinner.

They and their legal scholars had so corrupted the word of God.

Romans 3:19-26
Now, we know that whatever the law says, it says to those who are under the law, so that every mouth may be silenced and the whole world held accountable to God. Therefore, no one will be declared

righteous in his sight by observing the law; rather, through the law we become conscious of sin. But now a righteousness from God, apart from law, has been made known, to which the Law and the Prophets testify. This righteousness from God comes through faith in Jesus Christ to all who believe. There is no difference, for all have sinned and fall short of the glory of God and are justified freely by his grace through the redemption that came by Christ Jesus. God presented him as a sacrifice of atonement, through faith in his blood. He did this to demonstrate his justice because in his forbearance, he had left the sins committed beforehand unpunished he did it to demonstrate his justice at the present time, so as to be just and the one who justifies those who have faith in Jesus.

There is much in this parable that draws parallels to the Sermon on the Mount.

Luke 6:20-26
Looking at his disciples, he said, **"Blessed are you who are poor, for yours is the kingdom of God. Blessed are you who hunger now, for you will be satisfied. Blessed are you who weep now, for you will laugh. Blessed are you when men hate you, when they exclude you and insult you and reject your name as evil, because of the Son of Man.**

"Rejoice in that day and leap for joy, because great is your reward in heaven. For that is how their fathers treated the prophets.

"But woe to you who are rich, for you have already received your comfort. Woe to you who are well fed now, for you will go hungry. Woe to you who laugh now, for you will mourn and weep. Woe to you when all men speak well of you, for that is how their fathers treated the false prophets."

The two men's destinies were not caused by their worldly situation but belief or non-belief in the word of God and belief exercised in action / non-action. The rich man did nothing for Lazarus. He didn't abuse him or spit at him, but no mercy was shown. He showed him **no compassion**.

Matthew 25:41-45

"Then he will say to those on his left, 'Depart from me, you who are cursed, into the eternal fire prepared for the devil and his angels. For I was hungry and you gave me nothing to eat, I was thirsty and you gave me nothing to drink, I was a stranger and you did not invite me in, I needed clothes and you did not clothe me, I was sick and in prison and you did not look after me.'

"They also will answer, 'Lord, when did we see you hungry or thirsty or a stranger or needing clothes or sick or in prison, and did not help you?'

"He will reply, 'I tell you the truth, whatever you did not do for one of the least of these, you did not do for me.'"

The problem is not with lack of evidence but with a closed heart. Scripture is there for everyone to read. It is consistent, speaking about the Messiah and salvation. Note that Peter's first sermon (Pentecost—Acts 2:14-40) was grounded on scripture (Law & Prophets).

Hebrews 4:12&13

For the word of God is living and active. Sharper than any double-edged sword, it penetrates even to dividing soul and spirit, joints and marrow; it judges the thoughts and attitudes of the heart.

Nothing in all creation is hidden from God's sight. Everything is uncovered and laid bare before the eyes of him to whom we must give account.

2 Timothy 3:16

All Scripture is God-breathed and is useful for teaching, rebuking, correcting and training in righteousness...

What we do now determines our eternal destiny. We must know the word and understand the scriptures. We must live the word of God. The Law and the Prophets are summed up in the two great commandments:

Matthew 7:12

"So in everything, do to others what you would have them do to you, for this sums up the Law and the Prophets."

Matthew 22:36-40

"Teacher, which is the greatest commandment in the Law?"

Jesus replied: **"'Love the Lord your God with all your heart and with all your soul and with all your mind.' This is the first and greatest commandment. And the second is like it: 'Love your neighbor as yourself.' All the Law and the Prophets hang on these two commandments."**

We must be good stewards for God and use our wealth to help others. We should be careful not to decide destiny upon external appearances. Externalism gives rise to adapting religion to society. We are aware of the poor and needy. With the constant onslaught of the media, we cannot escape the reality and cannot claim ignorance. Let us not be like the rich man.

CHAPTER SEVENTEEN

T hings happen in life that cause people to sin. These are inevitable in our world. Anyone who causes another to sin, however, will be held accountable. Jesus used the imagery of tying a millstone around a person's neck and throwing him into the sea. The example played on the ancient fear of the deep and the real fear of drowning. So be aware. If your brother sins, rebuke him because you love him, and you want him to be see that he has sinned and that he recognizes his sin. Then he can repent and be restored to righteousness. Jesus said that if he sinned seven times in one day, and he repented seven times, you should forgive him. The illustration is meant to be extreme, with seven being the number for completeness, so regardless of how many times he sins and repents, you are to forgive him.

It is the apostles who understood just how profound this teaching was and how much faith would be required to live this way. It is no surprise then that their reaction was to say to Jesus, "Increase our faith!" To open oneself up to ask for help, to ask for the right thing, is a sign of spiritual maturity. They did not hesitate to expose their vulnerability to Jesus at this point. Because God was and is always ready to give us answers and gifts generously before we even ask for them, Jesus readily responded by opening their eyes to some truths about faith.

The mustard seed, as noted earlier (Chapter 13), is one of the smallest seeds. The point was obvious. If you have the tiniest bit of faith, you can accomplish great things. Faith in the power of God is to trust Him totally and be within His will. If that be so, then what is asked of Him is not limited and will be achieved through His power. Tapping into this supernatural power with the type of faith Jesus taught allows God's will to be done here on earth as it is in heaven. Great things that defy imagination can happen with faith.

Jesus elaborated on this relationship we have with God. When servants complete their work in the fields, they then must serve the master. It is only after they serve the master that they can take care of themselves. The first loyalty, priority, is to the master, God, and then to ourselves. The relationship is not questioned. Full, unhesitating compliance is expected. Even then, we are still unworthy. Why? Because we have received grace beyond what we deserve, and God continues to lavish love on us.

Luke, the storyteller he was, reminds us Jesus was on his way to Jerusalem and locates Jesus between Samaria and Galilee. A river ran along that border, along which they probably walked. The river made for easier travel, and there were towns on the way.

They were about to enter a village. In keeping with his penchant for the generic, so the lesson could be applied universally, Luke did not tell us whether the village was in Samaria or Galilee. In this case, omission was particularly pertinent in that they would be dealing with lepers. The law required that lepers were not to enter a town or get within six feet of other people, although most people would keep a much further distance from the lepers out of absolute fear. Thus, the lepers were isolated from society. By these restrictions, they were considered innately unclean and, of course, could not worship in the synagogue or temple. By default, they formed their own communities, erasing any prior social identities that may have prohibited their cohabitation. Ten lepers approached Jesus. He was standing at a distance, so they called out to Him for help, loud enough that they could be heard.

Jesus heard; Jesus saw; Jesus spoke. To go show oneself to the priest was the right thing to do under the Law after a healing so the priest could confirm the person was healed and was ready to be accepted back into the community. The ten were cleansed "as they went." One, realizing he had been cured, praised God loudly and returned to throw himself at Jesus' feet and thank Him. He was a Samaritan. No longer a leper, a Samaritan. Jesus asked the awkward question that everyone was thinking but afraid to say out-loud. Where are the other nine? The question implied the other nine may well have been Jews, since Jesus identified the one as "this foreigner." Metaphorically, this concept is consistent with Luke's perspective of the Jews' rejection of Jesus and the Gentiles' acceptance.

"Rise and go; your faith has made you well." Indeed, the man was healed in both body and spirit. Gratitude was and continues to be a necessary ingredient in faith.

The Pharisees were never far away. They tracked Jesus. They listened to what He had to say, some to learn more about what He was teaching and some to find something with which they could trap Him in violation of their understanding of the Law. He was under intense scrutiny. Luke traced their interaction with Jesus like a symphony, rising to a crushing crescendo in the mock trial prior to the crucifixion. The questions became more pointed, and the weight of the answers grew with each subsequent inquiry.

Now, the Pharisees asked Jesus about the Kingdom of God: When would it come? They had been trained to watch for the coming Kingdom. Scripture points to this Kingdom of God, and they and the legal scholars all debated endlessly about the signs that would show evidence of its arrival. Really, theirs was a legitimate question. Perhaps it was asked by a Pharisee who thought Jesus might know the answer.

Jesus' answer was the same, regardless of the motive behind the question. The truth was the truth. The Kingdom of God was not what they had come to believe it was from their studies and endless discussions. It was not a glorious savior, riding in on a grand horse with heaven's army to vanquish the occupying Romans and re-establish God's reign in Israel. It was not even anything substantive that could be seen or empirically validate. No, it was already there, though they did not recognize it. The Kingdom of God was a spiritual reality within their grasp. The true irony was that Jesus, the Son of God, stood before them, the incarnation of God Himself.

Jesus then turned to His disciples to teach them more. He looked into the future and told them they would seek for Him but would not find Him; they would seek for holy justice and comfort during the coming tribulations. Society would throw out many false messages. How true we now know that prophecy to be! But they would not need to be told where He was. When He does come, His arrival would be abundantly apparent, like a sudden blinding light across the sky. There would be no doubt. He told them again that first, He must suffer and be rejected.

He then gave two historical examples of what it will be like when he comes back. Life will be moving right along, people caught up in it, and suddenly everything will change completely forever, as when the great flood hit and when God struck down Sodom and Gomorrah because God executed His judgment. It will be likewise when Christ comes again.

Jesus now talked about "that day." The Day of the Lord, as foretold by the prophets and anticipated by the faithful. The day of judgment, when the righteous will be vindicated and the wicked punished according to their sins, when Israel will again be the people of God and Jerusalem His city. He will reside in His temple in David's City and rule all nations. These are the images His disciples would recall when Jesus referred to "that day."

A new element was added: the revealing of the Son of Man, a concept not new to scripture because Daniel told about this Son, but the prophecy was lost along the way (Daniel 7:13).

That day will happen suddenly, unexpectedly. Wherever they are and whatever they are doing, they should not turn back. There will be but that one opportunity, and there will be no doubt when the event happens. Jesus warned about turning back by referring to Lot's wife, who turned back to look at Sodom being destroyed as they were fleeing. After being told specifically not to turn around for any reason, she turned and lost her life. No, leave everything behind. Attempts to keep the old life will lose the opportunity for the new life. Regardless of how close people are, the selection of who will be taken will be based not on their similarities or kinships but on their relationships with God.

The disciples wanted to know where this event would happen, and Jesus simply gave them a provincial saying: watch for the signs of the times. These events will happen where necessary. The whole tone of Jesus' explanation was that of imminent actions.

CHAPTER EIGHTEEN

L uke unusually prefaces Jesus' next parable by telling the reader its meaning. Jesus told of a judge, who apparently cared about only himself. Judges were appointed by the Romans, and this particular judge was probably just a secular local, not in the Jewish circle, which suited the Romans fine. The second person was a widow, who was pressing a case, pleading for justice. She knew she could not depend on his sense of justice for relief because he did not fear God, so she continually pestered him. She was vulnerable and dependent upon the judge for mercy. Eventually, she wore him down, and he granted her wish, not because he cared but so he would not have to listen to her anymore. Her persistence paid off.

Jesus called him an unjust judge, and so he was. He did not acknowledge God, and even his ruling for the widow was not based on true justice but on selfish intent. The point, however, was that persistence worked with him. How much more would prayer work with God who longs to give His children what they want and need! The question Jesus asked, however, forced a different context to the parable. He referred to His second coming. Will His disciples be faithful up to that time? Jesus clearly implied a period of perseverance would be required. The real question becomes, not whether God will answer persistent prayer, but rather whether people will be persistent in their prayer. Will God's people be faithful in their prayers?

Once again Luke interjects his subjective comment to introduce the next parable in which Jesus contrasted two men praying in the temple. One was a Pharisee, who loudly prayed about himself, about how good he was. Notice how many times he used "I." The other was a tax collector, who stayed back, couldn't even look up, and begged God for mercy, acknowledging his sinfulness. Jesus made clear the tax collector went home justified—put into right relationship with God, forgiven.

The Pharisee was full of pride, the fundamental element in original sin. The tax collector, on the other hand, practiced humility. Jesus extrapolated the general lesson that those who exalt themselves will be humbled, and those who humbled themselves will be exalted. The lesson is like that of the seating at the dinner table, only Jesus elevated the lesson from a social level to a spiritual level.

"Don't bother the teacher!" The disciples viewed people taking young children ("babies") to Jesus as abuse of His grace and wasting His time. They thought they were acting in His best interest, helping Him manage His time, but Jesus redirected them and asked them to bring the children to Him. What an opportunity for a lesson! If you want to enter the kingdom of heaven, you must become like one of these, totally dependent upon God, fully trusting. Indeed, this type of simple trust is what God requires from us. Such surrender is natural for children and so difficult for adults.

Yes, children were looked down upon in society then, with no rights. Their mothers, though, loved them, and that's who would have taken them to Jesus for Him to bless. Stopping the practice would have prevented the mothers' access to Jesus as well and the benefit they derived by having their child blessed by Him. Jesus knew that. This story is another way Luke subtly shows how Jesus' loving ministry was intended for all, totally inclusive.

The next character Luke introduces us to is a rich ruler, which would place him in Jesus' travels toward Jerusalem. He probably had authority over some municipality simply because he owned most of the land in the area. His approach was somewhat unique, calling Jesus "Good teacher." Jesus immediately seized upon the title and asked why it was being used. Only God is good. All men are evil by their very nature. The twist in this response was that Jesus is, of course, good. Did this man recognize Jesus for who He was, or was the term mere flattery?

His question became the focus of the conversation. "What must I do to inherit eternal life?" Jesus listed the second table of the Ten Commandments, those that could be determined by one's outward conduct, with the exception of the last commandment. These, the rich ruler responded, he had followed all his life. All right, good. Jesus saw one thing in his way—his wealth. Jesus' instructions seem radical. Sell, give, and follow. He would, in turn, receive "treasure in heaven" and eternal life. Essentially, Jesus made him face the fact that he had not followed the last commandment, the one that many find the most difficult, not to covet. He had been holding tightly to his material possessions and was now being told to let go of them, a request that made him very sad. He realized he had not been completely faithful to God's commandments as he said earlier, and he would have serious difficulty following them all now.

Jesus knew his heart. He knew it's hard, very hard. To be rich requires certain attributes that by their nature make it difficult for one to enter into the Kingdom of God. One needs to have a minimal level of selfishness to be rich, which is antithetical to the principles of the Kingdom of God. Not that it is impossible, just very difficult. The rich also get to the point where they depend of their wealth instead of on God, which makes it harder for them to surrender. Jesus equates the difficulty to passing a camel through the eye of a needle, a typical middle-eastern hyperbole, but making the point just the same. Those who heard the truth understood it and asked who could be saved. They always thought the rich benefited from God; they received their riches because they had done good things, and God rewarded them. If the rich had a hard time getting into the Kingdom of God, then who could?

Jesus now closed in on his most important point: **"What is impossible for humans is possible for God."** Peter wanted to go back to the other point that had been made though and focused on the disciples' sacrifices they had made to follow Jesus. He was looking for assurance, and Jesus gave it to him. Yes, they had given up everything and would be rewarded, just as everyone now and forever who gives sacrifices for the Kingdom of God will be rewarded.

The disciples didn't really understand why Jesus was so intent on going to Jerusalem. They knew the Jews hated Him, and that was their capital. It was also far from Galilee, home. Jesus had told them twice before (9:44- 45, 17:25) His pending fate, but they didn't understand then. He took the twelve apostles aside and told them again. Even they, the inner circle, could not comprehend what He was telling them. They simply could not reconcile the concept of that kind of suffering with the image of the glorious Messiah they had been taught by their rabbis growing up.

Talking just to the Twelve, Jesus told them His destiny was the fulfillment of scripture. He gave them a specific outline of what would happen, but they could not comprehend it. Luke was not there. He received this information much later from those that were. How hard it must have been for them to tell Luke, to admit that Jesus had told them in detail what would happen, and that they did not understand (again)!

Their trip to Jerusalem now took them to Jericho, only 17 miles away from the holy city. As they approached Jericho, a blind man heard all the commotion and asked someone close to him what was going on. When he heard Jesus of Nazareth was coming through, he shouted out to Him. He called Him by His Messianic name, for he knew Jesus for who He was. Told to be quiet, he shouted out even louder, almost a primal scream. He was not going to let his chance slip by. He begged again for mercy. Speaking as a man with authority, Jesus ordered the man to be brought to Him. But when the blind man came close to Him, Jesus took on His usual servant attitude and asked what He could do for him. With the appropriate respect, the man simply asked to be able to see. With equal simplicity, Jesus granted his wish, telling him his faith had healed him. There was immediate healing, followed by praises to God as he followed Jesus. The crowd joined in with praises.

There are two great lessons from this event. The first is leading someone to Jesus; the second is healing through faith.

The blind man obviously had heard about Jesus of Nazareth, probably from travelers passing through Jericho. Who knows how much he knew and how much he learned from the Holy Spirit through prayer. He knew enough to believe He was the Messiah and to call out to Him in faith when he had an opportunity. In the meantime, he waited patiently. He waited for the Lord.

Psalm 40:1
I waited patiently for the Lord;
he turned to me and heard my cry.

Some would have prevented him from seeing Jesus. Society often puts up all kinds of barriers to prevent a nascent believer from getting close enough to become a convert, yet there is a primal need within us that calls out and will not be satisfied until we are saved. CS Lewis called this need a "God-shaped hole in our hearts." Taking one close to Jesus is enough. He will do the rest, relying on the inherent faith and the Holy Spirit.

Likewise, the healing. The man believed Jesus could heal him. Healing is much like prayer. God knows what we need before we ask and is more than willing and eager to answer our petitions. Here Jesus wanted to heal the blind man and as soon as he asked for his sight, he got it.

CHAPTER NINETEEN

A s Jesus entered and passed through Jericho, Zacchaeus entered the scene. He was, according to Luke, a chief tax collector. This term is not found anywhere else but probably denotes one in the hierarchy who had tax collectors working for him. Jericho was a major city of trade, therefore, a major tax center, implying that Zacchaeus would most likely have been a very wealthy man.

He might have been rich, but he was short. He wanted to see this Jesus of whom he had heard, so he climbed a tree to get a view as He passed by. Jesus didn't miss a beat. Just as He passed under the tree, He stopped, looked up, called Zacchaeus by name, and told him to come down immediately, that He must stay at his house that day. Jesus' statement was emphatic: This visit must happen. The apostles were probably astonished. Zacchaeus was overjoyed and took Him to his house. Zacchaeus just wanted to see Him; now, He was in his house! The crowd was not so happy. They saw Jesus as having made a very unwise decision by having gone to be a guest of a cheater, swindler, a Roman-lover of the worst kind.

Zacchaeus did the unexpected. He repented. He had a change of heart and life. Then he took action. He paid his debts—immediately. He actually went beyond double what was required by the Law by offering four times to anyone he had cheated. And forget about tithing! He gave half of what he owned to the poor. Jesus declared that salvation had come to his house, for Zacchaeus was a son of Abraham. In other words, he walked in the footsteps of Abraham—he was a true Jew. Why did Jesus make this statement? Because Zacchaeus complied with the **intent** of the Law through faith.

Consider:

> Ephesians 2:8
> For it is by grace you have been saved, through faith...

> Galatians 3:26
> You are all sons of God through faith in Christ Jesus.

> Romans 4:16
> Therefore, the promise comes by faith, so that it may be by grace and may be guaranteed to all Abraham's offspring—not only to those who are of the law but also to those who are of the faith of Abraham. He is the father of us all.

Jesus climaxed this extraordinary event with the statement, **"The Son of Man came to seek and to save what was lost."** This simple sentence summarizes Luke's Gospel. It succinctly captures Luke's perspective of Jesus coming to search through the world, including all people, and offering salvation to all, just as a shepherd sought out the one sheep. This statement helps explain how it was possible for the rich man to enter the Kingdom of God, for with God all things are possible. Jesus' summary declaration is the pivotal theological statement on which the whole gospel is centered.

Jesus' declaration to seek and save came after the stories of the blind man and Zacchaeus in Jericho. These two stories have much in common. Both men were desperate to see Jesus. Both took risks to see Him. The blind man kept yelling, thereby risking social ostracism. Zacchaeus risked his own life in public. Jesus invited both of them to come to Him and then rewarded their desperation. He also rewarded their petition, which had been offered in faith, spoken or not. Both men immediately took action after grace had been extended. The formerly blind man praised God and followed Jesus. Zacchaeus repented, repaid, and restored the social balance. Salvation was proclaimed directly and by praise.

While these events were going on, Jesus was still focused on Jerusalem. He knew where He was going, why He was going, and what would happen there. Others had quite different expectations. Their vision of the Messiah finally coming into David's City had been long nurtured by the Scribes and Pharisees, along with the rabbis and years of tradition and oral history. Their vision had only grown stronger with the iron grip of the Roman occupation. They were expecting glorious things. Jesus needed to again try and put some corrective lenses on them so they could better see the truth. He told them another parable.

Although the premise of the story may appear somewhat unusual, it was exactly what the Herods did when they became kings over Israel territories. Likewise, Jesus would also soon leave and return a king, though obviously no one there understood that.

The noble man in the story called his trusted servants, ten of them. These were the ones with whom he could entrust his estate while he was gone. He generously gave them the equivalent of four month's wages, a mina each. Each could do with it as he saw fit. The instructions were simple: "Put it to work until I get back." Whether he issued this instruction as a business practice or to test his servants is unknown; however, it certainly exposed their personalities, as we will see.

Jesus inserted an interesting statement here that the noble man's subjects hated him. Why we do not know. They were adamant, however, and went so far as to send a delegation to argue against his being made king over them. This effort failed. There was evidence of this type of resistance and its failure in Jewish history. Jesus may have included the reference to foretell of the Jews' reluctance to accept Him as their king.

After being crowned as king, the master returned and checked on his servants' productivity. The first servant actually multiplied the investment ten times! He was commended and given responsibility over ten cities. The king carefully phrased his praise for this servant. "Because you have been trustworthy in a very small matter, take charge of ten cities." Managing a mina of money was not really *a very small matter* when first faced with it. Being given four month's wages to work with for the master while he's gone would not seem like a trifle especially when it's you who had to manage it, and you know expectations were going to be high. The king, however, dismissed this duty as "a very small matter." His reward was greatly disproportionate to the money. The servant probably never guessed that there was even a possibility that he would end up responsible for ten cities! Suddenly, the money did seem small.

The second servant did very well too. He earned five times the principle and was given five cities.

One of the servants, however, took another path. He gave back the mina that had been given to him and offered what were clearly excuses for doing nothing. The king called him on the excuses, using the servant's own words to condemn him. The servant obviously didn't fear him, or he would have put the money in the bank. He simply did not care. He was totally apathetic. His excuses didn't even make sense. He didn't deserve anything, so the one mina he had was taken away. It was given to one who had exhibited responsibility and shown the ability to manage money properly.

The last verse (27) causes many concern. It does not seem like Jesus to them. Various commentators have interpreted this passage in different ways. Some say it is a reference to the future judgment when Christ judges the world. Others insist it is a direct reference to the Jews' rejection of Jesus as the Messiah, determining their own fate by doing so. Pilate did present Jesus to them as their king and was soundly rejected for doing so. "We have no king but Caesar!" the crowd shouted. Later, the Romans, to whom they had sworn allegiance, slaughtered the Jews in 70AD when they destroyed Jerusalem. Because the context of the parable is with the Pharisees present, the latter explanation does make sense.

The parable also spoke to the disciples. With the expectation of the imminent coming of the Kingdom of God, the disciples had preconceived notions about their roles (see Ch. 9—about who would be the greatest). This parable tells them that the coming times (of Jesus' being gone—to receive His kingdom from the Father) would not be a time of leisure and lordship but work. Even those who successfully managed their minas were rewarded with more responsibility.

Jesus now turned toward Jerusalem, the final leg of the journey He so resolutely began in Galilee. He knew there was a price on His head, and He knew the Grand Plan, but He also knew it was God's plan. He had been obedient to His Father's will all His life in every detail. Now, began the series of events that would inevitably lead to the climax of human history. He continued to prepare His disciples at every opportunity up to the last minute.

They left Jericho and headed to Bethphage and Bethany, just outside the city at the foot of the Mount of Olives. It was there that the Jews expected the Messiah to appear.

Zechariah 14:4
On that day his feet will stand on the Mount of Olives, east of Jerusalem

From this vantage point, on the hills across the Kidron Valley, one could see most of Jerusalem. The temple, its great walls rising hundreds of feet in the air, was on the east side, directly opposite the Mount of Olives.

Jesus carefully orchestrated His entry into the city. It was a deliberate claim to be a king. He was riding in on a donkey/mule/colt. In war kings rode horses; in peace they rode donkeys.

1 Kings 1:33-35
He [David] said to them: "Take your lord's servants with you and set Solomon my son on my own mule and take him down to Gihon. There have Zadok the priest and Nathan the prophet to anoint him king over Israel. Blow the trumpet and shout, 'Long live King Solomon!' Then you are to go up with him, and he is to come and sit on my throne and reign in my place. I have appointed him ruler over Israel and Judah."

Jesus was, in effect, saying, "Either accept me as king or reject me as king." This challenge was totally consistent with Luke's portrayal of his gospel. The truth was presented, and people had the choice either to accept it or to reject it, determining their fate by their decision.

A nice detail included by Luke, that the colt had never been ridden (or had never been used for work), which was a condition-precedent for consecration of an animal to God (Numbers 19:2, 1Samuel 6:7). The Lord who needed it was, of course, Jesus. Apparently that was enough for the owner. He understood the animal was appropriate for that use. Who was he to question?

The timing of Jesus entry was impeccable. Of course, it was God's timing, but everything aligned perfectly. In Daniel (Chapter 9) there is a rather complicated formula, which, if followed carefully, leads to the appearance of the Messiah at this time. It was normal for the prophets of old to enact dramatic presentations in order to illustrate the message they were trying to convey to the people. Ahijah tore his coat into twelve pieces to represent the twelve tribes of Israel. Jeramiah put on an oxen's yoke. Isaiah walked naked through the city for three days. Jesus now enters the holy city on a borrowed donkey.

The other important element to be considered in Jesus' timing of his entry was the annual entry of the Roman entourage each Passover. Each year, at this time when the city was swollen with pilgrims, they paraded into the city with full military regiment, with Herod Antipas riding a warhorse. Jesus intentionally rode a borrowed donkey and rode into Jerusalem on the opposite side of the city, illustrating a peaceful kingship alternative.

At least, the disciples understood the solemnity of the occasion and put their coats on the donkey for Jesus to ride on. The people recognized the symbolism and laid their coats on the road, preparing the way for royalty (2Kings 9:13). From that point on, crowd mentality took over and built. There were two crowds really. One group was the Pharisees, and the other group was the disciples. These disciples were both those who had been traveling with him and those who lived in Jerusalem. Many had personally witnessed miracles, plus there were the people of Jerusalem, some of whom had also seen miracles themselves and some who had just heard about them. The crowd frenzy continued to build to a crescendo. They were shouting "Hosanna!" which means "save now" but had become a colloquial shout of praise. Many quoted parts of Psalm 118. Everyone would be familiar with this psalm. They had to memorize it as part of required scripture for their bar/bat mitzvah to become adults. It was the song of special occasions in the temple and part of Passover and was sung by the pilgrims as they ascended the path that led to Jerusalem's gates.

The Pharisees took great offense in this treatment of Jesus, an itinerant rabbi from Galilee who had harshly criticized them. He certainly did not deserve this royal treatment. They asked Jesus to correct His followers. Theirs might not have been necessarily a hateful request. They knew the crowd's actions were inappropriate. Surely, Jesus knew, and He should reprimand them. They were violating convention. They were also concerned about the flagrant display, opposite the Romans' march, might be seen by Pilate as seditious. Jesus' response may appear at first to be another case of hyperbole, but it was based in scripture.

Habakkuk 2:11
The stones of the wall will cry out, and the beams of the woodwork will echo it.

The Pharisees would, of course, recognize this reference. First, God will be heard, one way or the other. Second, the reference to Habakkuk might have been indirect, but could have been the corruption within the temple. In the old prophet's time, his words condemned the Babylonians. Their homes were built with stones and wood they had plundered from others. These stones and wood would cry out against them at the time of judgment. Likewise, the stones of the temple would cry out against the corruption of the Pharisees and Scribes.

Jesus' lament over Jerusalem was heartrending. Here is the only place in Luke where Jesus cries. God's plan must be fulfilled. Even though the crowd was praising him now, another crowd in Jerusalem, less than a week later would call for His crucifixion. Jesus predicted the destruction of Jerusalem in 70AD by the Romans, which broke His heart. His reflections were reminiscent of His predictions of His second coming, where everyone was going about everyday life. Here, however, they were blind to the appearance of God.

When Jesus reached the temple, He was incensed by the moneychangers and merchants in the courts. They exchanged the currency brought in by pilgrims so people could buy the appropriate sacrifice for the temple. Yes, the process was necessary, but exchange rates were ridiculously high, benefiting both the moneychangers and the priests. Then, the cost of the sacrifices was exorbitant, taking advantage of the monopoly the merchants had. It was simply impractical to bring a sacrifice (a sheep, birds, whatever) long distances, so the pilgrims had no choice but to pay the high fees and costs. Jesus saw the social injustice of this system and gave them a taste of holy justice by driving them out of the courtyard.

Jesus' action immediately set Him against the hierarchy at the temple. He had attacked them in their purse. Not only that, He did so while quoting scripture. The reference to "house of prayer" was from Isaiah and "den of robbers" was from Jeremiah, two of the giants of the prophets. That they both preached strong and loudly about social justice might have touched a nerve with the temple Jews.

During His ministry, every Sabbath, Jesus taught at the local syna-gogue, wherever He was. Now, He was at the temple and could teach every day. He drew large crowds there, right under the eyes of the Jews who were trying to have Him killed. They wanted so desperately to get rid of the thorn in their side. He was upsetting their house of cards, everything they had carefully constructed to work within the existing political framework in order to maximize benefits for themselves. He was threatening all their plans. The people, however, loved Him. They loved what He said and the miracles He performed.

A few notes about the Triumphal Entry before we move on through Luke's book. It reads like a rather simple story, and those there saw it one way. Indeed, that was meaningful, but upon reflection, with the benefit of historic hindsight, we can see this event very differently.

Even at the surface, His entry didn't happen the way the people (and disciples) thought it would. Jesus rode in on a donkey rather than a horse, humbly rather than as a conquering king. He came not as a political revolutionary but as an emissary of peace. Even though Jesus had warned His disciples several times, as recorded in all the gospels, of His pending suffering, they totally forgot it at the time. The fame seemed so real, but Jesus knew what would happen. The event was itself prophetic:

Revelation 7:9-10:
"After these things I looked, and behold, a great multitude, which no one could count, from every nation and tribes and peoples and

tongues, standing before the throne and before the Lamb, clothed in white robes, and palm branches in their hands; and they cry out with a loud voice saying, 'Salvation to our God who sits on the throne and to the Lamb'."

The people then saw a conquering hero, a charismatic healer, a prophet, a political revolutionary. God saw a humble, obedient, suffering servant, His Son.

Consider the prophecy found in Zechariah:

Zechariah 9:9-11
"Rejoice greatly, O daughter of Zion!
Shout [in triumph], O daughter of Jerusalem!
Behold, your king is coming to you;
He is just and endowed with salvation,
Humble, and mounted on a donkey,
Even on a colt, the foal of a donkey.
And I will cut off the chariot from Ephraim,
And the horse from Jerusalem;
And the bow of war will be cut off.
And he will speak peace to the Gentiles [or, nations];
And his dominion will be from sea to sea,
And from the River to the ends of the earth.
As for you also, because of the blood of [my] covenant with you,
I have set your prisoners free from the waterless pit."

Here is Psalm 118, from which the people were citing from memory, the psalm so rich in quotable verses to us even today.

Psalm 118:
1   Give thanks to the LORD, for he is good; his love endures forever.
2   Let Israel say, "His love endures forever."
3   Let the house of Aaron say, "His love endures forever."
4   Let those who fear the LORD say, "His love endures forever."
5   In my anguish, I cried to the LORD, and he answered by setting me free.

6   The LORD is with me; I will not be afraid. What can man do to me?

7   The LORD is with me; he is my helper. I will look in triumph on my enemies.

8   It is better to take refuge in the LORD than to trust in man.

9   It is better to take refuge in the LORD than to trust in princes.

10 All the nations surrounded me, but in the name of the LORD I cut them off.

11 They surrounded me on every side, but in the name of the LORD I cut them off.

12 They swarmed around me like bees, but they died out as quickly as burning thorns; in the name of the LORD I cut them off.

13 I was pushed back and about to fall, but the LORD helped me.

14 The LORD is my strength and my song; he has become my salvation.

15 Shouts of joy and victory resound in the tents of the righteous: "The Lord's right hand has done mighty things!

16 The Lord's right hand is lifted high; the Lord's right hand has done mighty things!"

17 I will not die but live, and will proclaim what the LORD has done.

18 The LORD has chastened me severely, but he has not given me over to death.

19 Open for me the gates of righteousness; I will enter and give thanks to the LORD.

20 This is the gate of the LORD through which the righteous may enter.

21 I will give you thanks, for you answered me; you have become my salvation.

22 The stone the builders rejected has become the capstone;

23 The LORD has done this, and it is marvelous in our eyes.

24 This is the day the LORD has made; let us rejoice and be glad in it.

25 LORD, save us; O LORD, grant us success.

26 Blessed is he who comes in the name of the LORD. From the house of the LORD we bless you.

27 The LORD is God, and he has made his light shine upon us. With boughs in hand, join in the festal procession up to the horns of the altar.

28 You are my God, and I will give you thanks; you are my God, and I will exalt you.

29 Give thanks to the LORD, for he is good; his love endures forever.

CHAPTER TWENTY

J esus had only four days to teach in the temple, four days to teach to the people publicly in front of the Jewish hierarchy, the Sanhedrin. Most scholars believe the Triumphal Entry was on Sunday, thus Palm Sunday. Luke, in uncharacteristic fashion, introduced the next scene simply as "one day."

On this day, a consolidated group, each representing a contingent in the Sanhedrin, from the temple Jews approach Jesus to demand from Him his "papers." If He was going to come in as a king, complete with an ensemble of ambassadors, then He needed to be able to substantiate His authority. He had even exercised this authority on their turf by cleaning out the moneychangers and merchants from the temple courtyards right next to where He was now teaching. "Who gave you this authority?" The implication was that they came right up to Him, interrupting His teaching and demanding an answer. It was the same question they had asked John the Baptist.

Now it was common in a rabbinical exchange to return a question with a question. For example:

Luke 10:25-26
On one occasion an expert in the law stood up to test Jesus. "Teacher," he asked, "what must I do to inherit eternal life?" **"What is written in the Law?"** He replied, **"How do you read it?"**

Here, Jesus' question confronted the Jews and put the burden back on them in front of all the people. It was a legitimate question because many of the people did believe John the Baptist, and, of course, they knew John was a true prophet of God. The Jewish leaders were caught in a very uncomfortable position with no good answer. They couldn't afford to alienate the people, and they couldn't admit John's authority was divine, which would be to admit John had been right in his testimony that Jesus was the Son of God, the Messiah. Stalemate. So they lied and said they did not know. Truth requires truth, and they were not willing to pay that price. Jesus, therefore, was not obligated to answer the original question and chose not to, which exposed the lack of authority the questioners had over Him. In doing so, He avoided making a statement by which they could justify seizing Him.

While the temple leaders were still standing there, Jesus told a parable about a vineyard. As soon as He mentioned "vineyard," all ears were on edge. Vineyards were so often symbolic of Israel in the books of the Prophets.

Isaiah 3:14
The LORD enters into judgment against the elders and leaders of his people: **"It is you who have ruined my vineyard..."**

Isaiah 5:1-7
I will sing for the one I love a song about his vineyard: My loved one had a vineyard on a fertile hillside. He dug it up and cleared it of stones and planted it with the choicest vines. He built a watchtower in it and cut out a winepress as well. Then he looked for a crop of good grapes, but it yielded only bad fruit.

"Now you dwellers in Jerusalem and men of Judah, judge between me and my vineyard. What more could have been done for my vineyard than I have done for it? When I looked for good grapes, why did it yield only bad? Now I will tell you what I am going to do to my vineyard: I will take away its hedge, and it will be destroyed; I will break down its wall, and it will be trampled. I will make it a wasteland, neither pruned nor cultivated, and briers and

thorns will grow there. I will command the clouds not to rain on it."

The vineyard of the LORD Almighty is the house of Israel, and the men of Judah are the garden of his delight. And he looked for justice, but saw bloodshed; for righteousness, but heard cries of distress.

The man planted the vineyard. He started it from scratch. He had to have prepared the soil first, clearing it, weeding it, and tilling it. All life comes from God.

He rented it to some farmers, but he still owned it. Ownership always belonged to God. All Jews knew the Land belonged to God, and they were entrusted to be stewards of it.

At harvest time, the owner of the vineyard sent a servant to collect his share. God's timing is always right. The owner had been gone a long time, probably longer than the farmers thought he would be. They thought he might never be back, much like the mentality of modern Christians when they think of about the Second Coming. He asked for some of the fruit, his share, his tithe.

Leviticus 27:30
"A tithe of everything from the land, whether grain from the soil or fruit from the trees, belongs to the LORD; it is holy to the LORD."

Genesis 14:18
Then Melchizedek king of Salem brought out bread and wine. He was priest of God Most High, and he blessed Abram, saying, "Blessed be Abram by God Most High, Creator of heaven and earth. And blessed be God Most High, who delivered your enemies into your hand." Then Abram gave him a tenth of everything.

Genesis 28:20
Then Jacob made a vow, saying, "If God will be with me and will watch over me on this journey I am taking and will give me food to eat and clothes to wear so that I return safely to my father's

house, then the LORD will be my God and this stone that I have set up as a pillar will be God's house, and of all that you give me I will give you a tenth."

The owner sent three servants. Three is God's number (The Revelation to John). Not only were they sent away empty-handed, they were beaten.

Jeremiah 7:25-28
From the time your forefathers left Egypt until now, day after day, again and again I sent you my servants the prophets. But they did not listen to me or pay attention. They were stiff-necked and did more evil than their forefathers.'

"When you tell them all this, they will not listen to you; when you call to them, they will not answer. Therefore, say to them, 'This is the nation that has not obeyed the LORD its God or responded to correction. Truth has perished; it has vanished from their lips.

Acts 7:51-52
"You stiff-necked people, with uncircumcised hearts and ears! You are just like your fathers: You always resist the Holy Spirit! Was there ever a prophet your fathers did not persecute? They even killed those who predicted the coming of the Righteous One. And now you have betrayed and murdered him—

Next, he sent his son, his only son, the heir, (Both the Revised Standard Version and the New King James translations use "beloved son" which probably better conveys the meaning here), "Whom I love." Same words used at Jesus' baptism and at the Transfiguration. The Law stated that if the family were all dead, those in possession would inherit the property, so they killed him. The way Jesus phrases this, "They threw him out of the vineyard and killed him," might be a reference to the crucifixion just outside of Jerusalem.

What will the Father do? He will take life away from those who kill the Son. Life was His to give and His to take away. If He gives life to others, then it would be to the Gentiles because the Jews rejected the Son. The actual reference is found within Psalm 118:22, "The stone rejected by the builders is now the main foundation stone." The rejection of the Messiah would not thwart God's plans.

Oh, the people were definitely following what Jesus was saying! Kill the Jews and give what used to belong to them to the Gentiles? "May this never be!" But Jesus adds to the words of Psalm 118, Verse 22, with words better understood in the light of Isaiah's prophecy.

Luke 20:18
Everyone who falls on that stone will be crushed. And the stone will crush the person it falls on.

Isaiah 8:13
The LORD Almighty is the one you are to regard as holy, he is the one you are to fear, he is the one you are to dread, and he will be a sanctuary; but for both houses of Israel he will be a stone that causes men to stumble and a rock that makes them fall.

The fear of the people prevented the teachers and priests from doing anything, but they were incensed. Their frustration was a common theme until the last days of Jesus' life. The truth of God's Word was being exposed as never before, drawing a contrast that would culminate in history's most defining moment.

The tension between the Jewish leaders and Jesus had been building since Jesus came on the scene. From His first healing on the Sabbath until He cleansed the temple, His acts had been judged not by true righteousness but by what they deemed to be right according to the Law as they interpreted it along with their selfish agenda. As Jesus continued to exert His authority, produce miracles to help people, and teach parables that taught about a different understanding of God than they could comprehend, the leaders grew increasingly hostile toward Jesus. All His work appeared to undermine theirs and destabilize everything they had so carefully constructed over the years.

Recent events had brought their frustration to a climax. Though not recorded in Luke, everyone knew about the reported resurrection of Jesus' friend Lazarus that had happened not long ago and not too far from Jerusalem. Combined with all His past activities, the Triumphal Entry, and the temple cleansing, the leaders had reached the limit of their tolerance. It was time to take action and get rid of this problem.

The first approach was to trap him in public with a question, for which there was no acceptable answer. "Is it right for us to pay taxes to Caesar or not?" They intentionally asked a loaded question with logical fallacy built in. Of course, they prefaced the question with fine words (actually all true) to set the stage. Jesus had to be smiling inside, knowing what they were trying to do. The questioners, disguised members from the temple, figured Jesus would either greatly disappoint the people and tell them they must pay taxes or commit treason against Rome by saying they did not have to pay taxes. Jesus' response left them speechless.

The Sadducees then came to see Jesus. They were the aristocrats of the Jews, comprising the majority of the Sanhedrin. They did not believe in an after-life or resurrection of the dead. They also rejected the oral traditions of the Pharisees, along with the myriad of regulations formulated by them for the people to follow. They adhered to only the Pentateuch, the first five books of the Bible, written by Moses. They rejected Fate, which the Pharisees accepted, and believed in free-will. They rejected the concept of the Messiah. They also controlled the priesthood and were very powerful and politically-minded, compromising with secular authorities in order to remain in power. Through their compromises they represented the very worst side of the Jewish leadership.

It was very common for the Sadducees to debate theological questions among themselves. "How many angels could dance on the head of a pin" type of questions. So it was not unusual for them to approach Jesus with what appeared to be a legitimate theological question, albeit somewhat convoluted. It was interesting that the groundwork for their question involved resurrection and afterlife, neither one of which they gave any credence.

Jesus began with a given fact that everyone there knew and understood. People marry. He then gave them all new information. Marriage would not be a relationship in the resurrection or time eternal. It would not be necessary. There would be no more death; procreation would not be needed. Everyone there will be a child of God.

To substantiate the validity of the resurrection, Jesus cited Moses' references to God. No one would dare argue against Moses, the most revered of all prophets and the writer of the Pentateuch. This reference hit the Sadducees hard, for it was from the very scripture on which they leaned. The Scribes, listening to this exchange, applauded because Jesus had just proven their belief in the resurrection to be correct. Obviously, this revelation astounded the Sadducees as much as it delighted the Pharisees and Scribes. Both, though, were sufficiently intimidated by the depth of the logic that they refrained from asking any more questions of Jesus.

Now Jesus asked a theological question of them. He knew the Sadducees were on the ropes. One of their core beliefs had just been debunked, so He quickly attacked another by bringing up the Messiah. Jesus quoted from Psalm 110 (verses 42- 43) what appeared to be a paradox. How could the Messiah be David's son if David referred to Him as his Lord (master)? The answer would require the Jews to admit that the Messiah was the Son of God, not something they wanted to admit, especially in front of the people. This scripture also helped Jesus turn the conversation about the Messiah more toward its real purpose rather than the commonly held image of a militaristic savior. Even David would bow to this "son" as Lord someday as Master of eternity.

But Jesus does not stop there. With everyone still hanging on every word He was saying, He continued, turning to His disciples, He talked about the "teachers of the law." Unless they beat a hasty retreat that Luke doesn't tell us about, they were standing right there hearing all Jesus had to say. They were hypocrites and criminals! For their crimes, they would be punished severely. They would be punished more because they knew more and because they knew better. This teaching was similar to Jesus' teaching at the end of Chapter Twelve.

CHAPTER TWENTY ONE

L uke, the storyteller, says that Jesus looked up to see the people putting money into the temple treasury box. What a great segue! Jesus, always the one who saw what others didn't—watching and observing. There were thirteen boxes for putting money into, all in the Court of Women, open to all. They were shaped like large, upside-down megaphones (trumpets actually), which protected the money from theft. Each box represented a different type of offering, one for the wood, one for the incense, and so forth. The rich made a showing of their contributions, showering their money in to make the most noise possible.

Jesus used His observations as a teaching moment. The rich were giving from their spare change, money they could easily do without. The widow was giving from her heart, following the Greatest Commandment. Giving was not measured by what was given but by what was left afterward. Giving was measured by the sacrifice of the giver. She gave it all, trusting God to provide her needs. She had faith in God's provision.

The temple in which Jesus was teaching was magnificent. Herod had even contributed generously to its beauty. Josephus, the historian, wrote that it was beautiful; everything was either covered with gold or dazzlingly white. The disciples were remarking on the intricate detail. Jesus then warned them that everything they were looking at, including the massive stones that made up the walls, would all be torn down. Unfortunately, Jesus' prophecy would come true in just a few years. In 70 AD, the Romans totally destroyed the temple. The disciples now, however, asked when the destruction would happen and what would be the signs that it was about to happen. They felt they had a right to know.

Jesus told the disciples what to expect for themselves, in both the near and the far future. There would be those who mislead. Many wars and natural catastrophes would be a part of the world they would live in. The evidence of the language Jesus was using implied a crescendo of events. Then, He turned to the persecution of the church. His references clearly implied the universality of the persecution.

Persecution, however, yields opportunities. The disciples would become witnesses before kings and governors, places they would never have had access to otherwise. Then, they were to rely on the Holy Spirit for words to speak and wisdom that could not be resisted or contradicted. Their faithfulness would result in the spread of the gospel and their gain of eternal life. Such language Jesus used here is repeated in His revelation to John when describing the Seven Churches (The Revelation, Chapters 2-3).

Jesus now talked more specifically about the destruction of Jerusalem in 70 AD, an event most of the disciples would witness. The Romans would build ramparts around the walls of the city and put it under siege. During that time and the war that led up to it, over a million Jewish people died. Over 97,000 were taken in captivity, and the temple was totally demolished. Jesus used this imagery as a picture of the destruction of the last days. The Jews were to suffer, per the warnings God gave them when He gave them the Law if they did not abide in it. They suffered through the first exile in Babylon and now would suffer again for failing to recognize the truth in the prophets' words about God's Messiah. Jesus always said He was there to fulfill the Law. That the Jews refused to accept Jesus, would result in their condemnation. Luke crafts this message carefully and weaves these threads together, leading toward the Second Coming of Christ.

Jesus talked about natural phenomena that will occur, which humanity has never seen before. These will cause confusion. Things, which have always been stable, like the stars for navigation, will be shaken. It is then that Christ will come again. It will be with great power and glory. There will be no doubt about the event when it does happen. And when it does, the disciples should not despair but be joyful. Redemption is near.

The disciples were, no doubt, in shock at this point. All Jesus said was a lot to take in. They did ask, and Jesus answered, but they probably got more than they expected. As usual, Jesus was not perfectly clear. They would be turning His words over in their minds until they received help later from the Holy Spirit.

Jesus brought them down to earth a little, narrowing their focus by telling them a parable. One could tell summer was near by the leaves growing on all of the trees. Such a sign was easy for all to see. There would be no doubt about what was happening. That was the point. When the signs He had been describing climaxed, there would be no doubt. People would not be wondering if this were "it" or not. The power and majesty of the event would be so overpowering, they would leave no room for disbelief.

The next sentence Jesus spoke has been the center of much controversy. Many try to read into what he meant by "this generation." Or a better translation "this race." If Jesus was referring to the fall of Jerusalem, then the common term for generation would readily apply but that would appear to be out of the greater context. He was using Jerusalem's fall as the metaphor, albeit what will be an historical event, for the end times, but it was a small part of the portrait He was painting. It is equally unlikely Jesus meant that generation of Jews, as so many commentators subscribe. Yes, that thought would fit. They were promised by scripture that they would be alive until the end, but this was the same generation Jesus called "a wicked generation" (Luke 11:29) and "this adulterous and sinful generation" (Mk 8:38) because of its unbelief and unresponsiveness. "Yes, I tell you, this generation will be held responsible for it all." (Luke 11:51). The most likely meaning, and you probably had to be there to understand it, was that Jesus meant humanity from this epoch of history— from this time since the flood—this generation of people won't pass away until everything has happened. There will not be a premature ending of the world prior to the Second Coming of Christ.

So, the generation of humanity would not pass away until all these things had happened. Then Jesus added a corollary, **"Heaven and earth will pass away, but my words will certainly not pass way."** He was teaching them the true power of God's word. John, one of those listening that day, many years later, finally understood, and writing much later than the others, he wrote the preamble to his gospel:

John 1:1-14
In the beginning was the Word, and the Word was with God, and the Word was God. He was with God in the beginning. Through him all things were made; without him nothing was made that has been made. In him was life, and that life was the light of all mankind. The light shines in the darkness, and the darkness has not overcome it.

The true light that gives light to everyone was coming into the world. He was in the world, and though the world was made through him, the world did not recognize him. He came to that which was his own, but his own did not receive him. Yet to all who did receive him, to those who believed in his name, he gave the right to become children of God—children born not of natural descent, nor of human decision or a husband's will, but born of God.

The Word became flesh and made his dwelling among us. We have seen his glory, the glory of the one and only Son, who came from the Father, full of grace and truth.

Jesus himself was the Word of God. Here he actually was quoting from the Hebrew scriptures.

Isaiah 40:8
"The grass withers and flowers fall,
but the word of our God stands
forever."

The Word of God is greatly underestimated and misunderstood. With a word, God created the known universe; with a word, He changed human history; with a word, He empowered His church; with His Word, He provided salvation for all; and with a word, He will make all things new. All else is temporal, but God's word is eternal. We are the beneficiaries of His word in print through the books in the Bible, a precious revelation about God and His plan. Though the people who wrote were imperfect, the Holy Spirit inspired their writings, and the same Holy Spirit interprets those writings to us today. These truths do not change.

Yes, the Word is eternal; the rest of creation is just temporary, yet we live in this temporal world. Jesus warned His disciples of becoming so wrapped up in the day-to-day concerns of living, partying, and drunkenness that they become numb. Otherwise, on that day, the return of Christ would come totally unexpectedly. As He had warned them before, they needed to be ready, on watch, for that day will come to everyone on earth; no one will be exempt. "Watch and pray," He told them so they could stay alert, be strong, and withstand the events He had outlined. His lesson here gave another dimension to the end of the Lord's Prayer: "Let us not be led into tribulation." Perhaps Jesus meant the phrase to have the double meaning, to avoid temptation and to strengthen us against the coming tribulation should we face it.

Luke brings us back to the story, back to the scene. Jesus was teaching at the temple each day, and at the end of the day, He went to spend the night on the Mount of Olives, across the Kidron Valley from Jerusalem. The people rose early (very early) so they could get a good place to hear him teach the next morning.

CHAPTER TWENTY TWO

T he fear of the people had now built up in the Jewish leaders to a point where they felt compelled to get rid of Jesus in some way. He was increasingly popular. The people loved Him, but He was upsetting their world. The delicate balance they had managed to achieve with the Roman occupiers was based on the Jews being peaceful. This Jesus movement threatened to disturb that peace, especially if Rome sniffed a rebel in the midst. These are the dynamics as the Jewish leaders saw it, but there were also cosmic forces at work.

Satan returned to the scene and saw an opportunity to rid the world of Jesus by taking advantage of the Jews' hatred and exploiting the convergence of events. The Passover meal would take place a Thursday evening, the day before the Sabbath and in preparation for the Feast of the Unleavened Bread, which would last for the following week. Jerusalem would be full of pilgrims, almost twice its normal population. Normalcy was not the order of the day. In addition, one of the apostles had been weakening. Judas Iscariot had become increasingly dissatisfied because Jesus did not turn out to be the conquering king he imagined the Messiah should be. Satan always strikes at the weakest point. He prodded Judas, who then went to the Jewish leaders and offered to betray Jesus. They were thrilled and quickly made arrangements to pay him. The clear implication is that Judas asked for compensation. Interesting, really, for he was the group's treasurer. Apparently, his world revolved around money. (**"You cannot serve both God and Money."**) Now they just needed an opportunity.

Luke now begins to tell the events that lead from the Last Supper to the Resurrection. If the timeline of the book up until now has not been strictly chronological, the rest is. Luke is careful to note the movements of the critical players, when and where they did what. He starts with what is commonly called the Last Supper. This is the Passover meal Jesus spent with his disciples before his arrest. The earliest written description of this event is actually Paul's in First Corinthians. All four gospels include this scene and were written after Paul's letter. Paul, of course, got his information from those who attended when he visited Jerusalem after his conversion.

Jesus sent Peter and John to make preparations for the meal. The inner circle consisted of the two of them and James, John's brother. Jesus had this Seder well planned. The arrangements had been made in secret; not even the apostles knew what they were. The two sent were told only what they needed to know in order to accomplish what must be done. They were given an unusual sign. They were going into a city that was over-crowded and looking for one man. Men did not usually carry water. No one would know where they were. They would not be interrupted. Judas would have no opportunity to alert the authorities. Jesus wanted this time to be special, alone with His apostles. He wanted this time to be holy. He knew what He would do there.

In the secret room, Jesus reclined at the table with His friends, only the Twelve. He knew this meal would be His last one with them as well as His last meal on earth. He knew He would institute the ritual of the New Covenant that night with them, a ritual that would survive, not only the initial persecution of the church but also centuries of growth, change, dark ages, schism, reformation, and a plethora of denominations. The sacrament of Holy Communion stands to this day as an affirmation of the salvation found in the redemption of the sacrifice of Christ on the cross. He knew that then.

Jesus took one of the four cups used during the Seder to start. Here the "Kingdom of God" refers to the Second Coming of Christ. Then He took some of the unleavened bread and gave the traditional Jewish blessing, the same one He gave before He fed the multitude with five loaves and two fish. The broken bread is a constant reminder of Christ's sacrifice of His body for each one. Just as the manna was perfect and sufficient for each in the desert, so is Christ's sacrifice perfect and sufficient for each one of us. At the end of the supper, He used the last cup of wine as the establishment of the new covenant, His blood, poured out for all.

Hebrews 9:22
…without the shedding of blood there is no forgiveness.

The symbolism of the spilling of blood for the forgiveness of sins was familiar to everyone in the room. This was the very foundation of the sacrificial system at the temple, based on the Law of Moses. Each year, on the Day of Atonement, the high priest took one lamb for sacrifice for all the people of Israel and another on which he put all their sins—the scapegoat that was led out into the wilderness to be released. They all knew these things. Jesus made them understand that He would become the lamb to be slain for their sins. Yes, they would understand much more later, but this intimate experience would be the foundation of that understanding.

Now, Jesus shocked them. One of them was going to betray Him. Not only did they not understand who could possibly do that, but also they didn't even understand what He meant. He, the Son of Man, would follow prophecy, the will of God, the plan of God, because it must be fulfilled. He would be obedient to His Father because that is why He came. Even though Satan exercised his influence on Judas, Jesus warned Him of his terrible fate.

The disciples seemed to get over their concern fairly quickly though and launched into a dispute with each other over which one of them should be considered the greatest. Jesus scolded them. He has been teaching them servant-leadership by example for three years. The secular world used such hierarchy, even bestowing titles like "Benefactor," which Jesus seemed to use somewhat sarcastically. If anyone deserved to be the greatest, it was He, but He sat with them. He tried to reassure them. His Father had given Him all things, the Kingdom, and He had transferred the kingship to them. They would judge/rule in the future. In fact, they would act in that very role in the early church.

Jesus called Peter by his Jewish name, twice, for emphasis, and out of endearment, for Jesus loved this man He chose him to be the bedrock of his church. Satan would force trials upon all of them. They would be scattered. They would all return, except Judas. Jesus' prayer intervened. Peter, of course, objected. He was not weak. He would not fail. He was ready to go to prison or even die for Jesus. That's when Jesus told him that he would deny Him three times before the rooster crowed.

Jesus turned to the rest of the disciples to prepare them for their missions. The trip he sent them on before (Chapter 9) was a holy experiment. It taught the disciples much. They learned they could depend entirely upon God for all things while doing His work; He would provide. They had their first taste of the power of the Holy Spirit, even though they did not understand what it was, in healing and casting out demons. Their experiences brought them great joy.

Now, however, Jesus is telling them their missions will be different. They could not expect to receive hospitality on which they depended during their earlier trip. They would encounter rejection and outright hostility. They needed to be prepared, even to the point of being armed. As He so often has before, Jesus was speaking with hyperboles to make the point that the disciples would face fierce opposition. Of course, as usual, the disciples took His words literally and produced two swords to prove they are ready. Jesus cut them and the conversation off curtly with, "That's enough about that," probably frustrated that they still could not seem to grasp what He meant after all they had been through.

It was now very late, and Jesus headed back to the Mount of Olives with his disciples following Him. Entering the garden where they were staying, He told them to pray for themselves. Temptation was always at their door, but extreme circumstances were about to occur that would test them. They needed prayer to prepare them. He had already prayed for them, but His focused prayer now would be solely on Himself.

Jesus' prayer was simple yet profound. It illustrated the true nature of His humanity faced with the reality of God's plan, which He knew would involve torture, pain, and death. Jesus was familiar with crucifixion.

He had seen the crosses along the roadside and seen the men suffer, usually for days. He was only 33 years old and did not want to die. Everything in His humanness wanted to live. The will to live is the strongest survival instinct we have. Jesus, as a man, asked God if there was a way to accomplish His plan without this suffering, please allow that to happen.

Jesus had followed his Father's will all of His life. He also knew His plan. He knew the plan from before the beginning through the words of the prophets; it was in His blood. He knew why He was there, why He was born. He would submit to his Father's will.

The prayer is the perfect prayer. He asked for an alternative way if God was willing, but that He would be obedient to whatever God the Father led Him to do.

That only Luke records an angel came to strengthen Jesus during this time of extreme trial has intrigued many commentators. Some become concerned that this visitation might indicate His being lowered beneath the angels, and they lifted Him up. That's ridiculous. God has provided for His servants using angels, whether they be prophets or His own Son. They helped Him during His time of testing in the wilderness, and they helped Him now. As little as we know about angels, we should be careful in casting roles and hierarchy. God, the Father, was not averting the coming suffering but providing strength to endure it. Just as He prepares us for our challenges, here He prepares His Son for the ultimate test.

Jesus continued in prayer. He was in anguish, the term for extreme mental torment. It stressed him physically. He was sweating, and then his sweat became drops of blood. Rivulets of sweat ran off His face and dropped to the ground, terminology only our physician Luke would use.

Once Jesus had finished praying, He returned to find the disciples sleeping. They were overcome by grief and emotionally exhausted. Reality had started to set in, and it overwhelmed them. It was late, and they sought solace in sleep. They were not praying, as Jesus had told them to do, so He chastised them and told them to get up and pray "that they wouldn't give into temptation."

But there was no time for prayer. The opportunity had passed. Before they could draw another breath, the crowd arrived. Only Jesus had prayed, and over the next day, only He could resist the temptation that came.

The crowd was a motley crew, made up of a detachment of temple guards and officials sent by the temple chief priests, elders, and teachers of the law. They came with clubs and swords. Judas was with them, ready to give a sign as to who Jesus was so they could arrest Him, but there away from the adoring crowds. Jesus, still in command, preempted the signal. The disciples were now fully awake and realized what was really going on with the knee-jerk reaction of violence. An ear of the high priest's servant was cut off. Jesus, in full command, stops the action.

He healed the man's ear. His compassion knew no end. He practiced love to His enemies, just as He taught. He stopped the chaos and restored order, just as He calmed the sea. There would be enough chaos in the coming hours.

After a couple of rhetorical questions, the crowd seized Jesus and led Him away to the house of the high priest. It was night, so this would have been an informal interrogation by Caiaphas because the Sanhedrin could not meet at night. All the better to set a trap for Jesus and to gloat over His capture.

Caiaphas' house, his being a man of some means, would have a walled courtyard, also encircled by the house itself on two sides. It provided shelter from the wind and a semblance of privacy. Peter followed the crowd into the courtyard where they had started a fire to fend off the cool night air. Three times he was identified as being one of those who followed Jesus, and three times he denied their charge. A big, burly fisherman with a Galilean accent might be hard to miss. Each denial was stronger than the one before. At the last, the third denial, the rooster crowed. Jesus, knowing what was developing in the courtyard just outside the window turned and looked straight into Peter's eyes. Only Luke documents this gaze between the two, which tells us he learned these details from Peter. Peter then remembered Jesus' prophecy, ran outside, and totally broke down.

The soldiers, with Caiaphas' apparent approval, engaged in some crude horseplay—a rough version of blind man's bluff. If He were a prophet, then He should be able to tell who hit Him. Their game quickly spiraled out of control.

The meeting of the Sanhedrin had already been planned, based on the assumption that the arrest would be successful. They met early in the morning. This was the Supreme Court of the Jews, made up of seventy members. But there were no formalities, no pretense of a real trial. Jesus was led to the front and asked if He was the Messiah. It did not appear to matter to them that the Law said He could not be his own witness; His testimony would not be considered sufficient nor credible. They certainly were not about to answer His question.

Jesus correctly told them that if He claimed to be the Messiah, they would not believe Him. If He were to ask them, of course, they would not admit that He was the Messiah, even if some of them believed it. This was the turning point. When God is about to make a major change in human history, He tells humanity, "Look, I am about to do a new thing." Jesus told them, **"From now on, the Son of Man will be seated at the right hand of the mighty God."** The Sanhedrin immediately recognized this reference to Psalm 110:1 as a clear description for the Son of God, which is why they asked the next question.

"Are you then the Son of God?" Jesus answered clearly, **"If you want to put it that way, yes, I AM"** and He intentionally used I AM in His answer to remove any ambiguity. There was no doubt. The Sanhedrin needed no other witnesses. This Jesus had committed blasphemy in front of the whole assembly. They were all witnesses.

CHAPTER TWENTY THREE

T he whole assembly, seventy members of the Sanhedrin, temple guards, and Jesus paraded to Pilate's headquarters. There Jesus, accused of subversion, was presented to Pilate for judgment. Did He draw large crowds? Yes. Was He subversive? No. He was accused of refusing to pay taxes. Quite the contrary, in that He said to give to Caesar that which belonged to Caesar. The ultimate claim, however, was that He claimed to be the Messiah, which He did…which He was. That, they explained to Pilate, was a king. Yes, a king, though not the type these Jews thought the Messiah would be. A king that would threaten Rome? No.

Pilate's question was as much to humor the Jews as it was to quench his curiosity. "Yes," said this man who obviously had been beaten and was bound. In John's gospel, Jesus explained that His kingdom was not of this world. No wonder Pilate refused to find any reason to condemn him. He saw Jesus as no threat to Roman peace, the true litmus test for punitive action.

The Jews did not want to lose this chance. They knew they may never get another. They portrayed Jesus as being a widespread threat, all over Judea, coming here all the way from Galilee. Just the out Pilate needed. If Jesus were from Galilee, then let Herod deal with Him. That was his jurisdiction. He was in town for the Passover. How convenient, so Pilate had them take Jesus to Herod.

Herod was thrilled to see Jesus in person. He had been wanting to see Him and wanted to see a miracle. He also wanted to make sure this man was not John the Baptist reincarnate, as many had reported. But Jesus gave Herod nothing of what he wanted. He answered none of his questions, and He certainly performed no miracle for him. He had already been declared innocent by Pilate, so He just stood there.

Isaiah 53:7
… He was led like a lamb to the slaughter,
and as a sheep before her shearers is silent,
so he did not open his mouth.

Meanwhile, the Jews kept up their accusations. The soldiers joined in, put a royal-colored robe on Him, and mocked Him. Then they led Him back to Pilate. Apparently this farce played well with Pilate. He and Herod bonded through the affair, where before they had been enemies.

Pilate wanted to end this matter once and for all, so he called together Jesus' accusers and the people. Perhaps he hoped the latter would help balance their leaders' extreme views, knowing Jesus was popular with the people but who knew what made up the crowd that was assembled? Most commentators state that the same crowd that welcomed Jesus a week earlier now helped condemn him. With all the people in Jerusalem at the time, and the Jewish elders leading this effort, it was far more likely they rounded up a crowd of people who would support their views, perhaps even for some pocket change. Convicting Jesus was extremely important to the Jewish leaders, and they would do everything possible to accomplish their goal.

Pilate once again declared Jesus innocent of any crimes against Rome. He was willing to have Him scourged to pacify the Jews, even though it was illegal without a conviction of a crime. Flogging was nothing insignificant. The person would be tied to a post and whipped. The leather whip had ties on the end with pieces of bone, and lead chips. Forty-lashes would be the sentence. The executioner always whipped only thirty-nine times, for if he were to exceed forty, he would be subject to the same punishment. The results were gruesome, tearing the skin of the back off and causing massive bleeding. Many died.

There was an odd tradition that had developed between the Romans and the Jews during the Passover feast. The Romans would release one prisoner as a token of Roman generosity. It was on this basis that Pilate said he would punish Jesus and then release Him. The most notorious prisoner at the time was Barabbas. He had led a rebellion against the Romans and killed someone, two of the most serious crimes according to Roman rule. The crowd called for his release instead of Jesus'. Pilate would much rather release this indicted preacher than an enemy of the state. He appealed to the crowd again for some sense of reason. This attempt incited an increasingly loud response, for the crowd now called for Jesus' crucifixion.

Pilate regrouped. He tried one more time to present a logical approach to an ever-maddening crowd. The man had done nothing that deserved the death penalty. Why crucify Him? He repeated again his plan: flog Jesus and release Him. By this time, however, the crowd's hysteria was at its peak, encouraged by the Jewish leaders. They had been worked into a frenzy, reinforcing each other with continuing shouts of "crucifixion!" The last thing Pilate needed was a report to Rome of a civil disorder. He finally relented and took the path of least resistance, giving into the demand of the crowd. Barabbas was released, and Jesus was given over to be crucified.

We know from the other gospels that Jesus was flogged. Luke abbreviates this section and moves quickly on toward the crucifixion itself. On the way to the site, the criminal had to carry the cross beam on his back. Jesus, having just been flogged, would be too weak. He was probably barely able to walk. Simon from Cyrene was conscripted from the crowd to carry the beam behind Jesus. Cyrene is west of Egypt and had a large Jewish population. Simon was probably in Jerusalem, having traveled from Cyrene, for Passover. Although Simon was a common name, we know of this man from his sons Rufus and Alexander, who were active in the early church.

Every crucifixion drew a crowd. Usually, it was the morbidly curious. Jesus, however, drew a large crowd. Many were those who just a few days before, were joyfully welcoming Him into Jerusalem as the Son of David. Some were the usual lot, while others were from the crowd who forced His sentence. Many of those who wept were women. Jesus, weakened and bloodied, still had compassion for others. Quoting Hosea's prophecy, He referred to the fall of Jerusalem, not that many years away, when women who had no children would not have to see their children suffer through that catastrophe. The devastation was still heavy on His heart. If this barbarous act was what happened when the Messiah is on earth, what would it be like when He was gone?

Jesus was then crucified, along with two common criminals, at the place they called the Skull, Calvary, probably just outside the city gate. Whether it was called that because the hill resembled the shape of a skull or because it was a place of execution, we don't know. Maybe both. It was on the way into town so everyone could see, an example of Roman justice. As Isaiah foretold:

> Isaiah 53:12
> Therefore, I will give him a portion among the great,
> and he will divide the spoils with the strong,
>
> because he poured out his life unto death,
> and was numbered with the transgressors.
>
> For he bore the sin of many,
> and made intercession for the transgressors.

Crucifixion was the most painful method for torturing and killing someone the Romans had devised. It usually took two to three days to complete. The person's wrists were nailed to the cross beam, and one nail was driven through both feet. The legs were left slightly bent so the person could push down on them, though painful, necessary in order to breath. If a quicker death were desired, the legs were broken, making it impossible to breath. Death came in many ways but usually by dehydration, bleeding to death, suffocation, or simply failure of the major organs due to stress.

Jesus was fixed to the cross and lifted up into place.

> Numbers 21:9
> So Moses made a bronze snake and put it up on a pole. Then when anyone was bitten by a snake and looked at the bronze snake, he lived.

John 3:14

"Just as Moses lifted up the snake in the desert, so the Son of Man must be lifted up, that everyone who believes in him may have eternal life."

Jesus finally spoke. He had everyone's attention. He prayed aloud and asked His Father to forgive them because they do not know what they were doing. Forgiveness. The essence of the gospel. Here Jesus interceded, even under the most extreme of circumstances.

Hebrews 7:25
Therefore, he [Jesus] is able to save completely those who come to God through him, because he always lives to intercede for them.

Acts 7:59-60
While they were stoning him, Stephen prayed, "Lord Jesus, receive my spirit." Then he fell on his knees and cried out, "Lord, do not hold this sin against them." When he had said this, he fell asleep.

Ephesians 4:32-5:2
Be kind and compassionate to one another, forgiving each other, just as in Christ God forgave you. Be imitators of God, therefore, as dearly loved children and live a life of love, just as Christ loved us and gave himself up for us as a fragrant offering and sacrifice to God.

Jesus asked for forgiveness, even for ignorance. The Roman soldiers crucifying Him had no idea who He really was, much less the part they were playing in God's plan. They were doing their job. They got to share in whatever paltry possessions the criminals had, which usually was just their clothing, so they cast lots, fulfilling Psalm 22, "They divide my garments among them and cast lots for my clothing."

Now that they got what they wanted, the Jewish leaders mocked Him, saying that if He was truly the Messiah, He would have been able to save Himself. They had completely rationalized the justification for killing Jesus.

John 18:14
Caiaphas was the one who had advised the Jews that it would be good if one man died for the people.

The soldiers joined in, illustrating the partnership between the Roman authority and the Jewish leaders. This group was indeed the establishment that the Jews were working so hard to protect. The delicate balance that allowed them to keep their world as-is while under Roman occupation. These soldiers mimicked the Jews. They all still would have loved to see a sign. The soldiers teased Jesus with wine vinegar, the drink of Roman soldiers.

Over His head was written His crime for which He deserved to be crucified, according to Pilate: "THIS IS THE KING OF THE JEWS."

Even one of the criminals being crucified with Him joined in the mocking, tying the Messiahship to salvation, saying that if He was the Messiah, then He could save them. The other criminal, though, saw things differently. He feared God (the beginning of wisdom) and wondered why the other didn't. In that truth, he recognized that they had committed crimes for which they deserved crucifixion, but Jesus was innocent and did not. He confessed and then asked Jesus to remember him when He came into His kingdom. He trusted Jesus to do the right thing.

Jesus, ever full of mercy, emphasized His answer ("I tell you the truth") that the man was forgiven and would be with Jesus in paradise.

From noon until 3:00, there was darkness. The curtain separating the Holy of Holies was torn in two, signifying the barrier broken forever between God and humanity, providing direct access to all. Even Jesus' last words were scripture, taken from Psalm 31, verse 5—trust from a righteous sufferer. Then Jesus died. His human body had suffered torture to the extreme of its failure. Born as the Son of God, His Father allowed Him to die to atone for all the sins of humanity. Only this One would suffice, the perfect Lamb, innocent, sacrificed to end all sacrifices. His fate was part of God's perfect plan to reconcile humanity to Himself. But make no mistake, Jesus gave up His life voluntarily at His time. He, the

Author of Life, was always in control, and it was He who decided when His human life would end.

This redemptive act is the Ultimate Truth that sets humanity free and provides free access to eternal life for all. Without this sacrifice, all else is meaningless.

> 1 Corinthians 1:23-24
> but we preach Christ crucified: a stumbling block to Jews and fool-
> ishness to Gentiles, but to those whom God has called, both Jews
> and Greeks, Christ the power of God and the wisdom of God.

The centurion in charge had seen many die on the cross, yet Jesus' death was remarkable, extraordinary. The events were so powerful that those present were shaken, leaving them beating their chests in sorrow. Those who knew Him watched in agony, including the women who had supported His ministry all the way from Galilee. They could safely be there and witness these events.

Joseph of Arimathea was one of those, like Simeon and Anna who welcomed the young Jesus, who eagerly anticipated the coming of the Kingdom of God. He was one of the Sanhedrin who refused to vote with the majority. Imagine the courage it took for him to go to Pilate and ask for Jesus' body! It was late in the day. Given the time of year, it would be almost dark. Being Friday, that meant that the Sabbath was about to begin, so he had to work very quickly. He wrapped Jesus in linen and put him in a new tomb. The women watched, saw what Joseph did, and then went home to get things ready to prepare the body properly as soon as the Sabbath was over.

There is nothing in Luke about the Sabbath, the day between the death and the discovery of Jesus' resurrection. It was the one day in history when God was quiet. The Word was silent.

CHAPTER TWENTY FOUR

The first day of the week was Sunday, the first day in which work could be performed after the Sabbath. The women, determined to prepare Jesus' body properly, left very early in the morning and went to the tomb where they had seen his body laid. Each tomb had a large stone rolled in front of its entrance. The stone would be rolled into a small crevice in the ground, which was usually carved out of rock, and land hard into it. Moving the stone would take three to five strong men working together. Luke does not tell us how the stone was moved, about the Roman soldiers being posted at the entrance, the Roman seal placed on the stone, or many of the details found in Matthew's or Mark's gospels. He simply says the stone had been rolled away.

But why was it moved? We know it was not so Jesus could leave the grave. Information Luke and others provide later tells us—the Glorified Christ was not constrained by physical boundaries. No, the stone was moved solely to allow his followers to look inside and see that he was gone.

The women were intent on their mission and go inside, but they did not see the body. They were confused. Before they could collect their thoughts, two men suddenly showed up. They are identified by Luke as men, but their garments were remarkable—gleaming white, brighter than bright. The women were overwhelmed. First the stone had been moved, then Jesus was gone, and now these very unusual men with magnificent clothing suddenly appeared! In the typical human reaction to an encounter with the divine, they showed fear and bowed down.

What words of reassurance they heard! He was not dead but living! His resurrection was according to the plan, which Jesus had told them previously. Actually, Jesus had shared the plan with His disciples five times: Luke 9:22, 9:44, 12:50, 17:25, and 18:31-33. They didn't understand then, but now they could understand.

The women returned to the apostles, now the Eleven, and told them what they had seen and heard. Mary Magdalene was always named first when a list of the women followers is given. Joanna was the wife of Cuza, and this Mary was the mother of James and John. Their talk came across to the men as foolishness. The term Luke uses here to describe the women's story is one a doctor would use of a patient, "babbling from a fever."

Peter, on the other hand, jumped up and ran to the tomb. He had his own reasons of course. He had never lost his impetuous nature and needed to see the empty tomb for himself. Peter had personally experienced fulfillment of one of Jesus' predictions and desired to observe firsthand the fulfillment of this prophecy as well. Amazed, finding the empty tomb and the linen cast aside, he departed "muttering to himself." Not to be lost, however, is the fact that by going and seeing the same thing the women did, Peter became a second witness, verifying the facts of the event.

The following section (verses 13-35) is found only in Luke, commonly called the Walk to Emmaus. Cleopas and a fellow disciple were walking from Jerusalem to Emmaus, about seven miles, an easy day's walk. They could now make that walk because the Sabbath was over, so they traveled together, walking and talking about all the events of the past week.

Along came a stranger. They were kept from recognizing Him as Jesus. Here and as in the other gospels it was common for people readily not to recognize the risen Christ as Jesus. They eventually did, and for each there was a different sign that opened their eyes. Jesus was there, but until they were touched in a personal, spiritual way that linked them directly to Jesus, they did not see Him for who He was.

The usual pleasantries were exchanged, and He joined them in their conversation. Curiously He appeared to be oblivious to the recent events that had taken place in Jerusalem. They were incredulous. We might have asked, "What planet are you from? We're talking about Jesus of Nazareth, a great prophet, powerful in word and deed before God and all the people."

Indeed, this Jesus is the one they had expected to liberate Israel from its oppressor, Rome. After all, wasn't this what they had learned the Messiah would do when He appeared? Sadly, all their hopes had been dashed when their religious leaders conspired to have Him killed three days ago. That meant His soul would have already departed his body. In addition, to add to their confusion, women from their inner circle had gone to Jesus' tomb that morning, only to find it empty. Their stories were a mix of unbelievable fantasy about angels, saying He was alive! Incredible stuff, too crazy to believe. One could see angels in a vision but not really see them in a real setting. Especially peculiar was that all of them saw them together. Of course, men immediately went to check the women's story, only to find the tomb empty and the body gone.

At this point, Jesus, the risen Christ, casually walking with his disciples, was frustrated. All His teachings appeared to be lost on them, even in light of the overwhelming evidence validating His own prophecies. He calls them fools, a term He had previously reserved for the Pharisees and Scribes. Didn't these disciples listen when He told them exactly what would happen? Didn't they recognize that what had just happened was what He had foretold?

So Jesus taught them again. He took them through the scriptures: Moses (the Law) and all the Prophets, covering the entire known Hebrew scripture. He interpreted God's plan and how everything led to His Suffering Messiah.

As they approached Emmaus, Jesus kept walking as they turned to go into town. It was getting late, a dangerous time to be traveling alone. The two men urged him to stay with them. He joined them at the table, and their eyes of understanding were opened when Jesus broke the bread and gave thanks, something they had seen Jesus do many times. The memory broke through their spiritual daze. It was as though the Holy Spirit put glasses on them, and they saw Jesus for who He was. Once they recognized Him, He vanished. They then understood why their hearts were stirred when Jesus had explained the scriptures to them. The Holy Spirit was indeed at work! It took the interpretation of the Word of God and the breaking of the bread to change this man from a stranger to Jesus the Christ. Even though it was now night and unsafe, they immediately went to Jerusalem to tell the Eleven what had happened. They found them gathered with other followers celebrating because Jesus had appeared to Peter. Then they told their story! He was risen indeed!

Everyone was excited, they were all talking to each other, and **suddenly** Jesus appeared. His greeting was the common one used by all at the time, yet the reaction was anything but calm. To hear these stories and contemplate the possibilities is one thing, but for Jesus Himself just to show up abruptly was another. He knew their hearts, as He always had, and tried to reassure them that it was He and not a ghost. To help prove His point, He ate some fish in front of them.

Jesus then taught them, like He had Cleopas and his friend on the way to Emmaus, about all the Hebrew scripture. Their minds were opened so they could understand His teaching. They were being prepared. His good news was to be preached to all nations, beginning in Jerusalem. They were to teach what He had been teaching during His three years of ministry—one must have a change of heart, and then there would be life for the forgiveness of sins.

They had been witnesses to His ministry and now were to be witnesses to others. He would equip them as He had promised, so He instructed them to stay where they were until they became endowed with this heavenly power, which would enable them to preach this good news to everyone.

This promise foreshadows the coming of the Holy Spirit at Pentecost, which Luke writes about in the Acts of the Apostles. Here, Jesus was promising His disciples a new thing: one of the Great Promises of God— **He faithfully promises His presence.** As modern Christians, we take this promise for granted, but for them, this was a revolutionary concept. God would be with them, living within them, all the time! Jesus had been living with them for about three years, the I AM in human form, Immanuel, but now it would different. Each one of them individually would be endowed with the power of the Holy Spirit, living and breathing the life of God.

Jesus led them all out to Bethany, the place where the scriptures say the Messiah would come. After His blessing, He was taken away. There was certainty, closure, finality, but there was no mourning. Instead, the disciples, for the first time, truly worshiped Jesus. They were overwhelmed with joy.

Luke leaves us with the disciples continuously praising God with joy in the temple. Luke started his gospel in the temple and appropriately finishes it in the temple.

www.ingramcontent.com/pod-product-compliance
Lightning Source LLC
Chambersburg PA
CBHW071338090426
42738CB00012B/2936